WALKING THE RELINQUISHED PATH

By
Michelle Wedel

Sweetgrass Press L.L.C
P.O. Box 1862
Merrimack, NH 03054
http://www.sweetgrasspress.com

Copyright © 2002 by Michelle LaVigne-Wedel. All rights reserved.
No part of this book may be reproduced in any form or by any electronic or mechanical means including information and retrieval systems, websites or Internet without permission from the publisher in writing.

Library of Congress Control Number: 2002090579

Michelle LaVigne-Wedel 1962 -
Walking the Relinquished Path

ISBN 0-9714272-8-3

ORIGINAL COVER DESIGN: The Electric Wigwam

Editor: Paul Wedel

Printed in the United States of America

Address all inquiries to:

Sweetgrass Press L.L.C.
P.O. Box 1862
Merrimack, NH 03054
USA

URL: http:// www.sweetgrasspress.com
E-mail: info@sweetgrasspress.com

Dedicated To:
My Mish-oh-miss (Grandfather) for all he has given me, including such a perplexing and challenging puzzle as is my search.
And to my Ancestors, both Native and European, for giving me the thread of life.

TABLE OF CONTENTS

Preface.. I
Chapter 1.   A Child's Story....................... 1
Chapter 2.   What's An Indian.................. 18
Chapter 3.   The Tangled Clues................ 31
Chapter 4.   Uncle Bob's Mystery............ 40
Chapter 5.   My Not So Cunning Plan..... 56
Chapter 6.   What's In A Name................. 63
Chapter 7.   Wings Of White Eagle........... 80
Chapter 8.   The Internet Path.................. 91
Chapter 9.   The Connection..................... 115
Chapter 10. Real Indian............................ 136
Chapter 11. The Shame In The Shell........ 144
Chapter 12. The Gift Of The Fox.............. 152
Epilogue... 158

> **Please note,** some of the names in this book have been changed at the request of family or out of respect for the privacy of others.

Preface

As I write this preface, my country — the United States of America — is at war in Afghanistan, fighting terrorists who are threatening to take away the way of life we celebrate in the United States. Our attackers have committed the most hideous of crimes against humanity. They now threaten our people with biological weapons sure to kill thousands if they succeed. They see us as a terrible evil, even the personification of Satan here on Earth.

How could anyone think this way, we ask ourselves. We tell our children that our way of life is good and true, and that we will survive and stop the terrible attackers. We look at what our attackers believe about us, and what we know about ourselves, and find it hard to understand how different the two views are. We wonder how any people could let their belief become so perverse that they would wish to commit genocide in the name of their God.

How many of us fail to see that this is merely history repeating itself?

Consider the following quotes. Someone living today could easily imagine a Taliban terrorist

WALKING THE RELINQUISHED PATH

speaking them in regards to the current people of the United States:

"...put a most effectual stop to their very Being" [1]

"...that Vermine ... have forfeited all claim to the rights of humanity" [2]

"…try every other method that can serve to extirpate this exorable race." [3]

"…we gave them … blankets and an handkerchief out of the small pox hospital. I hope it will have the desired effect." [4]

"What can you expect from filthy little heathens? Their whole disgusting race is like a curse. Their skin's a hellish red. They're only good when they are dead!" [5]

      The first four quotes came from men who helped settle New England. Actually, there are several towns named after these men. For example, Lord Jeffery Amherst has towns in both Massachusetts and New Hampshire named after him. There is even a university that carries his name. His claim to history? Controlling the terrible Indian scourge, thus making New England safe for the white settlers.

      It causes me great pain to drive to the nearby town of Amherst and think that such a beautiful, quaint New England town represents the legacy of such a demon of a man. I call him a demon, yet he was known as a hero by the people who believed he was doing God's will and helping Europeans obtain their "Manifest Destiny" over ***their*** land that just happened to be infested with Indians, some of whom were my ancestors.

The premeditated and systematic killing of the ancestors has become one of the most painful things I have learned. Before I read deeply into the colonial text, I was like most people I know. I knew that the Indian people had been given a bad rap. They had land taken away, and that they were not happy about their lives on reservations. After reading some of the colonial texts and records, I discovered a totally new view of the suffering the Indian's endured. I understood, if only perhaps a little better than before, the reasons behind the feelings expressed by the aboriginal people today. More importantly, I realized why my grandfather did his best to impress upon me an extremely deep shame and fear of my traditional roots, and his own intense fear of his true heritage.

My grandfather's fear, and the political policies that have created it, have become the biggest roadblock I have had to dig through in my quest to follow the path relinquished by my ancestors.

The systematic killing of the indigenous people of America was so effective and so complete, that many tribes of people were entirely wiped from the face of this Earth. Their culture, their ways, their beliefs, their language, their hopes, their dreams —

WALKING THE RELINQUISHED PATH

everything about them is gone. There are no records. There are none who remember their stories. There is nothing left of these people. Surely, even the dodo bird was documented by the people of that time before the last one died. Odd that the people of the day felt more need to preserve the ways of a bird than of a race of human beings.

Of the tribes who managed to survive through the terrible biological attacks and other methods of genocide, few are whole and complete in their traditions and beliefs. Few have been able to keep pure what makes them who they are as an individual people. So many died without handing down knowledge of their traditional ways, medicines and stories. Many more were pressured and persuaded by missionaries into giving up what they believed. Some did this because they came to believe in the missionaries' ways, some because they realized that it was the only way to survive.

Many of the surviving tribes were methodically indoctrinated into a world where being a native was such a terrible prospect that they would do anything, including lie, bribe and falsify records to try and pass for English, French or any other nationality, so long as they were not thought of as Indian.

The few tribes who have managed to stay intact still struggle. The fear and pain of the wrongs done to them — many of those wrongs done not so long ago that there are still elders alive who remember the pain — continue to haunt them. They still must face the continuing problems at the hands

Preface

of their self appointed benefactors. In addition, the relatively new trend of non-native people looking to embrace the Indian's belief system as if it were some magical solution for all the troubles of the modern world has put pressure on tribes to keep what they have of their culture and belief pure and strong, despite the insurgence of non-Indians who, in their ignorance, apply a generic view of the native people's culture and spiritual outlook that is quickly becoming a new stereotype.

It is this web of complex issues that create the obstacles and pitfalls most will face on the path to discover their Native American ancestors. It is the pain and fear created by these issues that caused our ancestors to relinquish the path they walked.

---

1. Letter from Lord Jeffery Amherst to Sir William Johnson 1763
2. Letter from Henry Bouquet to Lord Jeffery Amherst 1763
3. From the reply by Amherst to Bouquet's letter 1763
4. Journal of William Trent, excerpt:[May] 24th [1763]
5. Song: "Savages" from the Disney movie "Pocahontas"

WALKING THE RELINQUISHED PATH

Chapter 1
A Child's story

To say that my life has always centered around my need to know about my Indian past would be a bit of an exaggeration. Yet, it was always there as part of my life, to some degree or another. The stages of my life greatly affected not just my feelings about my native blood, but how those around me influenced those feelings.

The first major stage was my early childhood. Until about age seven or eight, my grandfather talked openly to me about his people and their ways. This was a wonderful period in my life. My grandfather and I were the best of friends as he shared his secrets with me.

The following is a narrative based on a typical summer during this stage of my life. The events recalled are actual and as close to how I remember them as I am able to record. Although the exact dialogue is obviously re-created, it reflects what I recall being said, at least in meaning, if not in actual words.

WALKING THE RELINQUISHED PATH

A Child's Story

Michelle woke up early, like she always did in the summer. She climbed out of bed, jumped into her play clothes and opened up the door of the little camping trailer which was home for the summer months. She hurried outside to be greeted by her grandmother and grandfather, or Mimere and Pipere as she knew them.

"You ready for breakfast?" Mimere asked. She poured some pancake mix on the hot griddle and in no time at all Michelle had a plate full of golden pancakes. She ate them quickly before her brother Tommy got up. She knew if she were ready to go before her brother woke up, Pipere would take her with him. Pipere would not want to take Tommy, because he was too young, and Mimere would insist that both children go, or neither one goes.

Luckily, both Michelle and Pipere finished their breakfast before Tommy woke up.

"I'm going for my morning walk," Pipere said. He stood up and stretched. "Coming with me, Kitten?" He motioned for Michelle to follow.

"Coming!" She hurried happily behind him.

They walked from the campground through the deep woods that stood behind it. They stopped now and again to pick small orange flowers that grew low to the ground. Pipere showed the child how to crush the flowers and use the crushed petals

Chapter 1

as a balm to keep away the mosquitoes that were rather heavy in the deep woods.

They walked through a dry, barren area that appeared to the child like a slice of the Sahara desert right in the middle of the forest. Pipere stopped and picked up some bluegreen moss that was growing on the ground. "Look for some of this," he said. "It does a lot of good things. We can even use it to start a fire tonight."

Michelle picked moss and showed it to Pipere. The moss she picked seemed flakier and more white than blue.

"No, this is not the right stuff." Pipere took the moss from the child and placed it carefully back on the rock where she got it from. "It is more blue and soft like velvet. Pick the dry stuff, leave it alone if it feels like a sponge."

The child tried again, this time getting a few dry bits of velvet-like, blue moss. "Here, Pipere. Is this the right stuff?"

"You got it, Kitten!" Pipere smiled. He took the moss and put it in his pocket. "Now go get some more."

"It's hot out here in the sun," the child complained. "How much moss do we need?"

"Just enough," Pipere said. Pipere always gave times and quantities in vague statements like, "just enough" or "until we are done." This perplexed the child. What seemed even stranger was that before too long, she came to understand exactly how much is "just enough" or how long it would be "until we are done."

WALKING THE RELINQUISHED PATH

Once they had "just enough" moss, they continued to walk. Pipere pointed out some other trees and bushes as they walked. He said some were good for making medicine to stop coughs and explained that every bug in the forest could be eaten. "If you ever get lost in the forest," he said, "you would have a lot to eat. Lots of bugs live in the forest."

The idea of eating bugs didn't thrill Michelle. "Yuck, I wouldn't eat bugs."

"You would if you were hungry," Pipere said. "That is, if you didn't get enough berries in the summer time." As he spoke, Pipere bent over and began to pick dark blue and purple berries from the low lying wild blueberry bushes around his feet.

Michelle joined him and began to pick the berries, too. "Pipere, there are so many berries. How can anyone in the forest go hungry?" She picked a handful and ate them happily. They tasted so good, better than any store bought blueberry ever could.

"Today there are a lot of berries, but what about tomorrow? What about in the winter when the bushes don't have berries?" He filled a small bag he carried with him full of the perfect little spheres. "What do you do if you want to eat berries and it's the winter?"

"Go to the store and buy some?" the child replied.

"When I was a boy, there were no stores. When we wanted berries in the winter, we had to

Chapter 1

make sure that we picked enough of them in the summer and saved them for the winter."

"When you were an Indian kid?" she asked.

"Yes, when I was an Indian kid." He smiled.

"How did you save berries, Pipere? Don't they go rotten?"

"You have to dry them so they are like raisins. You need to lay them out to dry and you have to keep the birds away from them." He filled his bag and began to walk away.

"Did I ever tell you that you can make dye for clothes from blueberry skins?" He walked up a hill to another grove of wild berry bushes. This bunch had thorns, and Pipere cautioned the little girl to be careful not to get pricked.

"I love raspberries!" Michelle said as she ran headlong into the bush. The thorns scratched her arm and she started to bleed.

"See, I told you to be careful," Pipere said. He walked over to a small plant with pointed leaves. He broke off a leaf. White sap dripped from the stem end. Pipere dabbed the sap on the scratch. "All better?" he asked.

"Yes. All better," the child replied. "What plant was that?" she asked.

Pipere told the child the plant's name. As soon as he said it, she forgot it.

"Remember," he added, "Never, *never* eat this plant. Never eat it." He emphasized by waving the leaf in the little girls face.

"I won't," she said.

WALKING THE RELINQUISHED PATH

"This plant you can eat." Pipere picked a dark almond shaped leaf from a little shiny plant that was growing on the forest floor. He broke the leaf in two and put it in his mouth. He offered the child the other half. She smelled it. It smelled wonderful; just like the yummy chewing gum her grandmother gave her when she helped clean the kitchen. She put the leaf in her mouth. It was minty and sweet, despite the strange texture it had on her teeth.

After Pipere had picked "just enough" raspberries, the walk continued to a nearby pond.

"Be very quiet when we go to the water," Pipere cautioned. "If you are quiet, we might see a moose by the water's edge and we can talk to him."

"But the leaves keep crunching. We can't sneak up on anything." She pouted.

"Yes we can. Our people knew a way to walk in the woods so no one would hear them." He bent down to look at the little girl directly, face to face. "I will show you, but you have to promise never to tell your grandmother."

"Why?" she asked innocently.

"Because your grandmother doesn't like me to teach you about the Indians," he explained. "So you have to promise you won't tell her that I talked about our people."

"Ok, Pipere. But if we can't talk about them, how come you call them our people?"

Pipere cringed. He knew any answer he gave her would probably lead to more questions. Pipere

Chapter 1

thought for a moment and said, "Being Indian is a secret."

"Why?" the child persisted.

"Because it is. Now do you want to learn how to walk quiet in the woods or not?"

"Oh, yes!" she said. "Please!"

"Alright then. Do what I do." Pipere carefully put one foot out, toe first, into the leaves and twigs. Carefully, he parted the larger of the sticks with complete silence. Then he cautiously placed the ball of his foot down in the slightly cleared area. He gently moved his foot from side to side, then in total silence, placed his heal down onto the forest floor. Not one leaf dared to rustle. Not one stick snapped.

Using the same method, he followed with his other foot. After demonstrating several times slowly, he walked into the woods at a quicker pace, barely making any sound at all.

"Now, do what I did," he instructed Michelle.

She took a deep breath and began to imitate her grandfather's steps. It took her several attempts to try and clear the leaves before she put the ball of her foot down, but each and every time the leaves rustled. Still, the child was undaunted. She tried again and then stepped down. "Snap!" A twig on the forest floor gave way. The child tried again and again, but her attempts at walking silently were far from successful.

Pipere gave her a harsh look as leaves rustled beneath her feet. But as she approached, his scowl turned to a smile and he said, "That was good. You keep practicing and soon you will get it."

They walked to the water's edge; Pipere silent as midnight, Michelle quite a bit louder. When they got to the water's edge, Michelle pouted. "I must have scared away the moose," she said sadly.

"The moose are not out this time of day," Pipere said, if only to console the child.

When they got to the edge of the water, Pipere picked some of the long grasses that were growing on the edge of the shore.

"What is that for?" Michelle asked.

"This stuff?" Pipere snapped the reeds in the air as if they were part of a giant grass whip. "This is just about one of the most useful things you can have. You can make rope from it. You can tie things together with it. You can do a lot of things with it." Pipere handed the girl some of the long strands. "Take this in your hand like this and sit down."

Michelle sat on a rock by the water and held the grass between her palm and her thumb like her grandfather instructed.

"Then roll it on your leg like this. When you get near the end, add a few more grasses in." He quickly rolled the long reeds tightly on his thigh, then added another few blades of grass as he came to the end and began to twist them into the first. "You keep adding and adding until you have it as long as you want. When you have some long strands made, you can even roll them together to make thicker rope."

Chapter 1

Michelle rolled the few original grasses and did her best to roll the new strands in as she got to the end of the first threads. They slipped out and unwound when she pulled on her newly made rope.

"Well, it takes practice, too. Besides, this grass is still wet," Pipere said with amusement.

"We can bring some home to the campsite and let it dry. Then I can practice," Michelle said as she gathered more grass.

"No. We can't do that," Pipere said sternly.

"Why not?" the child whined.

"Because then your grandmother will know we talked about it. Remember, this is our secret. If you want to practice you have to go to the water alone and practice where no one can see you."

"But no one will let me go to the water alone. They say I'm too little," Michelle reminded.

"Well then, we will have to just practice when we go for walks." Pipere rolled some more grass into rope and began to tell Michelle a long story about how the grass came to be. The child was amazed by the story. Then Pipere told her stories of the different grasses and what each one does and how they came to do what they do. He told her stories about animals who behaved a lot like people. He told her stories about his life as a child in Canada with the Indians. And when his stories were all done, he showed her how he made his newly formed rope into an animal snare and how it could be used to catch a rabbit or a squirrel. But he didn't use his snare. Instead, he tossed the grass rope snare into the nearby bushes.

WALKING THE RELINQUISHED PATH

"Pipere," Michelle asked, "what was the name of our Indian people?"

"I think they would call you Kitten," he said. "And they would call your little brother Chicken Wings!" He laughed so loudly, his laughter echoed across the lake.

"But what is the tribe name?" she asked again.

"You don't need to know that," Pipere said, then announced it was time to get back to camp.

The walk back to camp wasn't as fun as the walk into the woods. The conversation on the way back was not happy at all.

"Okay, soon we will be back at the campground. If anyone asked what we did you know what to tell them," Pipere said to the child.

"Yes. I tell them we went for a hike to the lake to fish." Michelle looked at her empty hands. "But we didn't take the fishing poles this time."

"Never mind about that." Pipere thought for a moment. "If someone asks, we can just tell them we got to the lake and remembered that we forgot our poles, so we came home."

"Why not just tell them we went to the lake to see if we could find the moose so we could talk to him, and when he wasn't there, you showed me how to make rope from the grass?"

"No!" Pipere said sternly. "Decent people don't talk to moose. And decent people buy rope at the hardware store!"

"But Pipere?" Michelle stopped walking and looked up at her grandfather. The old man continued

Chapter 1

to walk. Michelle sighed, then ran after him. "Pipere. Why are Indians not decent people? You used to be an Indian!"

Pipere stopped in his tracks and looked down at the child. The pain in his eyes was easy to see, even for the small girl. "Used to be," he said with emphasis. "When my father became Catholic, we were not Indian anymore. We became Catholic. If you are a Catholic and you go back to being an Indian, you're going to burn in hell. You understand that?"

"But why? I think being Indian is good if you are an Indian. Why can't you be an Indian and be a Catholic Indian? Why would God be mad if you made rope from the pond grass or talked to the moose?" she asked with the innocence of her age. "If God made you an Indian, why would He be mad at you for it?"

"Because people don't like Indians!" Pipere said with a voice so stern it made the child shake. "People think Indians are less than dogs! They treat Indians worse than they do black people. If you tell anyone you're an Indian they won't let you go to school. Your friends won't be allowed to play with you anymore and everyone will think you're always drunk and lazy!"

Michelle stepped back, her eyes rimmed with tears. "But Pipere, how come?"

"Just because!" he said firmly. "So you don't tell anyone. You hear me? Anyone! If you do, they will take you away and put you in a school for

Indian kids were they will beat you and make you eat trash they can't feed to pigs!"

The vision of such a place filled the child's mind. Often her grandfather talked about the terrible ways Indians were treated. He talked at length about how "they" let Indian children starve to death rather than even let them eat the scraps "they" tossed to their dogs. He told stories of how "they" chased Indians out of stores when the Indians wanted to go shopping, and how "they" made Indians pay more than twice as much for anything the Indains bought. He told her how "they" would not let the Indian's have jobs no matter how hard the Indians worked. He said that no matter if an Indian never drank a drop, "they" would call him a drunk.

She had no idea who "they" were, but suspected, based on the way her grandfather talked, that "they" were everywhere, watching.

"I promise," she finally said to Pipere. "I won't tell anyone we are Indians."

"Good," Pipere said. For the remainder of the walk to the campground he did not say another word.

When they arrived at the campsite, Pipere handed the child the bag of berries they had collected. She ran to her grandmother and gave her the bag. "Here Mimere, can I eat them now?" she asked, not mentioning how many she ate in the woods.

Mimere took the berries, rinsed them with water, put them in a bowl and called Tommy out to help eat the berries.

Chapter 1

Michelle and her brother began to fill their mouths with berries, and Mimere went off to tend to some other chore. Pipere also walked away to do some chore.

"Tommy, guess what?" Michelle said to her brother between mouthfuls of the berries.

"What?" he asked.

"Pipere showed me how to make rope from that long grass that grows at the sides of ponds," she bragged.

"That's not fair!" Tommy yelled. "You always get to do the fun stuff."

"What are you fighting about?" Mimere called over. "If you don't share the berries I'll take them away."

"Yes, Mimere," Michelle said.

She turned her attention back to her little brother. "You can't tell anyone. Remember. It's an Indian secret!"

"But it's not fair!" Tommy whined. "Pipere always tells you everything. He never takes me out in the woods. It's not fair!" he shouted again.

"What is going on?" Mimere came over to see what the commotion was.

"Nothing," Michelle said. She hoped her brother would follow suit. He didn't.

"It's not fair!" he complained. "Pipere took Michelle into the woods and told her how the Indian's make rope and stuff like that. He never takes me."

Walking the Relinquished Path

"I see," Mimere said. Her face took on a furious look. "Fred!" she shouted at the top of her lungs.

Pipere appeared to come from nowhere. "What? What's the matter?" He rushed to the table to see what was wrong.

Mimere turned to her husband. The fury was easy to see in her eyes. "You! You!" she fumbled her first few words in her anger. "You stupid old man!" she finally managed to shout.

"What?" Pipere slouched his shoulders as if he didn't know why she was angry.

"Your grandson here is mad because you didn't tell him how to be an i.n.d.i.a.n." She spelled the word as if saying it would curse her.

"Oh, come on," he moaned, "it was just a little fun. That's all. I only showed her some plants. Nothing terrible. Just kids stuff."

Mimere slammed her hand down on the picnic table that stood in front of our little camper. "You know I forbid you to talk to the kids about that nonsense! You're going to fill their heads with that terrible stupid stuff!" She motioned for the children to go into the camper. Once they were inside, she continued talking in a more quiet manner in hopes that the children wouldn't hear her.

"What are you doing? You know better than to talk to the children about your being Indian! You want them to get thrown out of Sunday school?" Mimere scolded her husband.

Pipere sat at the table, head hung low. The sorrow he was feeling was clear on his face. Inside

Chapter 1

the camper, Michelle felt like crying as she watched her grandmother yell at her grandfather. Guilt filled her when she realized that if she hadn't bragged to her brother, then her Pipere wouldn't be in trouble now. She thought to herself that Pipere looked like he was about to break into tears. She began to cry, herself.

Outside of the camper, Mimere continued to batter her husband with endless words about the shame and pain he was exposing the children to. She continued on about how she would die of embarrassment if any of the children ever told someone she knows that their grandfather was an Indian.

Finally, after what seemed to Michelle to be hours of endless words, Mimere said in a sharp vicious voice, "I better never have to tell you again, Fred. You keep your no good mouth shut about your dirty Indian blood! Bunch of no good drunks the whole lot of those damn Indians!"

Pipere got to his feet and quietly walked back to what he was doing. Mimere called the children from the camper and told them to go play in a nearby playground.

Tommy ran to the playground, but Michelle lagged behind. She looked at her grandfather, now so crestfallen, looking so much older than she had ever seen him look before. She wanted to go up to him and tell him she was sorry for telling the secret, but she knew he would not talk to her about it. That was his way. He didn't talk about what made him upset. He didn't talk about his feelings. She knew this, so she just looked for a moment longer then went to join her brother at the playground.

As Tommy ran and played around her, Michelle sat quietly on the hard wooden swing and looked back at her Pipere. He sat by the firepit, breaking small pieces of wood into even smaller pieces of wood. There was no fire going. He reached into his pocket and took out the handful of bluegreen moss she had helped him collect that morning. He looked at the moss and mumbled something. She didn't have any idea what, because he was too far away for her to hear.

"Maybe he's going to make a fire with it," she said quietly to herself, remembering what he said in the woods about it being useful for making fire. She leaned forward on her swing as if trying to get a better look.

Pipere looked up then down at the moss one more time, then tossed it into the woods with an angry, abrupt motion. Then, in the same angry abrupt way, he got up and walked off into the woods towards the campground bathroom.

"Pipere! Can I come!" Michelle shouted and ran after her beloved grandfather. He didn't turn. Perhaps he didn't hear her. "Pipere, can I come with you!" she called again.

He looked back, then paused to let the child catch up. "Sure Kitten," he said. "But I'm only going to the toilets."

"That's ok. I have to go, too," the child lied with a smile. She was just happy to be with her grandfather.

Chapter 1

Pipere laughed and they walked together into the woods toward the little cement building that housed the men's and ladies' bathrooms. They only paused once so Pipere could point out a certain tree and how to use its leaves if you get a bee sting.

Chapter 2
What's an Indian

Growing up with my grandfather held a lot of mixed messages. On one hand, he would show me the most amazing things he remembered from his boyhood with his people and tell me long stories about amazing creatures and animals who lived on the big island he said America was part of. He also told me some strange stories that not only amazed me, but frightened me at times about monsters and mysterious beings who had amazing powers.

On the other hand, he would tell me never to speak to anyone of what he told me and by the time I was nine or ten years old, he did a full reversal on me and stopped talking about our people all together.

At that point, when I asked our about his people, even the most simple or innocent of questions was met with short, curt answers denying he ever said anything or that he was even an Indian.

During that time, he told me stories about his family coming from England, France, Ireland and even Mexico! When I dared to point out the inconsistencies in his tales, he would just tell me I was being too nosy and to leave him alone.

Chapter 2

But once in a while, when the mood was right, my grandfather would talk to me about his Indian roots and stories about what it was like growing up.

Whenever he told his stories, he was always careful to make sure no other adults were around. He knew that if any adult in our family heard him talking about the subject, he would be told in no uncertain terms to shut his mouth and not fill our heads with things that would only get us in trouble.

Some of my grandfather's stories about his growing up were rather amazing and they helped shape my idea of what his people must have been like. Yet, the way he behaved, the obvious shame he had and his endless warnings to never tell anyone we had indian blood in us sent such a confusing message.

Then, if only to mess up my already confused opinion, there was the media. It was the sixties. A time of change and free love for some, but for me — a child of less than ten years old — it was endless TV shows. Many of them were reruns of things like "Howdy Dowdy", "Buffalo Bob" and other cowboy shows. On the weekends, my father would take over our TV set to watch endless hours of old John Wayne movies where the blood thirsty savages killed the innocent people of the west who were just trying to make a living.

I heard people in these movies saying things like, "The only good Indian is a dead Indian." I watched as the God fearing hero rounded up and shot the Indian men who obviously had IQs below room temperature because they couldn't talk in more than one syllable words and only knew how to kill and make war.

I began to think, "No wonder people hate Indians. All Indians do is kill people."

Then I thought about my grandfather. How loving he was. I could never imagine my grandfather hurting a soul. How could my grandfather be an Indian?

I began to understand why my grandfather was afraid that people would treat him differently if they knew he was an Indian — but little did I know how different that would be. I had no concept of the true prejudice and hatred my grandfather and his family had to face.

I once asked my mother — who is my grandfather's daughter — why everyone was telling me that no one likes Indians. She answered, "Because Indians don't believe in God."

How could that be? I was Indian, at least partly, and I believed in God. My mother was half Indian and she believed in God. My grandfather was all Indian and he believed in God.

I asked my Father the same question. My father said, "People don't know Indians. That's why they don't like them. If you get to know people who are different, you find out you have a lot to like about each other."

This really confused me. My father was from a long line of French Canadians. He had no Indian blood at all in him. He didn't seem afraid of the topic, nor did he seem to dislike Indians. Why

Chapter 2

was my father, the representative of the non-native side of my family, the only one who had anything good to say?

I tried to believe what my father said. The reason people don't like Indians is because they don't know them. But it was hard. In addition to my own families seemingly prejudice views, as I grew older, I became more and more aware of how the media portrayed Indians.

I started to become afraid that if I did tell people I was of Indian blood, they wouldn't want to get to know me and see how alike we were, as my father had explained. But rather, they would think I was like the television Indians who killed the nice pioneers in the movies. What if my friends decided that I was bad? What if my grandfather was right when he told me that if my friends found out I was an Indian, they wouldn't want to play with me anymore? What if I could never go to school? What if my family was thrown out of their house and out of the city? What if I was shot by some cowboy?

You might think these thoughts were silly, but I assure you, these are the types of issues I had to deal with as a child.

Being an Indian was the family shame. It was hard for a child to understand why. These silly ideas were my attempt at understanding why the family was ashamed and afraid of anyone knowing about my grandfather's roots.

What added to the difficulty was that despite the negative stereotypes I was being bombarded with, and the terrible warnings issued by my grandfather every time I dared to speak of it, I wanted more than anything else to know about who these people were who could make rope from grass and heal cuts with sap from a leaf. I wanted to know more, because I could feel them inside my heart. Sometimes the feeling and need was so strong it hurt too much to even think about.

I lived in a world of strong mixed messages that were in direct conflict with my inner need. I dreamt the most vivid reoccurring dream through my childhood that today I link directly to this conflict of my inner self and my surrounding environment. The dream was always the same. I dreamt it well over fifty times, perhaps more, from the age of about 8 to 12 years old. It was at times a nightly dream.

It always starts that I am standing in my backyard. I am alone. I am approached by a white dog, which I greet and pat happily. Then I notice a white horse standing in the yard. I walk up to the horse and it motions for me to get on its back. I climb on the animal and it rears up on its hind legs. As it does, it grows so large that I can see over the roof of my house. Then it jumps into the sky and I can see over the houses in the neighborhood. It flies to the forest where it lands and I get off where I am greeted by many people. Some have very little clothes on, but most have white animal skins on. They are very happy to see me and I feel like I am home. For the first few moments when I wake from this dream, I feel so far away from home and alone.

Chapter 2

I knew that the people in that dream were my grandfather's tribe. I also knew that somehow they were calling to me. But why?

Dreams of strange and marvelous white animals have been a constant in my life since I can recall. Perhaps they were planted there by my grandfather's wonderful stories. Today, I have no memory of his actual stories of the animals, but I still have the dreams from time to time.

So, who where these people? What were Indians? Were they good or bad? Did they have to be either? My grandmother was married to one. Maybe she would know.

I got my nerve up and asked my grandmother about her opinion of Indians. It was not flattering in the least. So I asked why she married an Indian man if she disliked Indians so much. The following is the story she told me:

She said she was not what you would call a really young girl when she met my grandfather. She saw that he was a hard working man and she thought, based on his last name, that he was Irish. His family name was Shaughnessy. Though she spoke only French and he spoke little French they got along well and decided they would be a good match for each other.

My grandmother didn't speak of love very often. I always figured it was because she had hardened her manners and outward show of affections due to the hardships of raising a family during the depression. It was not surprising to me that she didn't mention love as one of the criteria by which she and my grandfather got together. Love was a word she never said very often, but rather something she put into all the cooking and knitting she did for the family.

She talked about how when they first got married, my grandfather took a job out of town and she only saw him one weekend a month. She said her brother complained to her that her husband was always out of town. Her brother suggested that if he could get her husband into his fraternal lodge, the fellows there could help him find a much better job that was closer to home. So it was decided, and her brother nominated my grandfather for membership in his fraternal lodge.

"You should have seen your grandfather when I told him," she explained to me. "You would think I was asking him to take up with the devil himself!"

She said he began to make excuses for not joining the lodge. He even tried to say his religion forbid it. But she pointed out it was a lodge that the Catholics did not disapprove of. Besides, it was already done. Her brother had already put in the nomination and there was going to be an interview coming in the next few weeks.

She explained that after a few weeks, her brother came back to her and told her that my grandfather had been turned down. "Black balled" was the termed she used.

She wanted to know why, because he was never even interviewed. Her brother told her to sit

Chapter 2

down. Then he said, "Marlene, you married an Indian."

My grandmother's eyes opened wide as she told me about how shocked she was. She recounted with a tone that still carried the taste of her initial shock, how she told her brother to stop lying and stop talking like that about her husband. She said she didn't believe him. It was too terrible to believe.

As she told me this, my heart broke inside. How could being an Indian be so terrible? I dare say she would have seemed less shocked if she were told he had only six months to live.

She said that when my grandfather got home, she told him what her brother said and pleaded with him to tell her it was just a vicious lie.

My grandfather told her it was not a lie. She made him promise never to tell anyone about it ever, and she made her brother do the same.

Her eyes seemed far away in the memory for a moment, then she looked at me with all seriousness and said, "If I had known he was an Indian, I would have never married him."

"What?" I was now the shocked party. "Wasn't he still a good worker and provider? Didn't you still make a good match? Don't you love him?" I asked.

"Of course, of course," she said. "I love him." She paused.

"Well, if you love someone it shouldn't make a difference, should it?" I persisted.

"Maybe times are different now. But back then it made a difference. If people found out he was an Indian, me and my kids would be trash in everyone's eyes. How could I let that happen?" She looked at me. "You would be trash, too, if anyone knew."

I didn't know quite what to say. After a few awkward moments my grandmother changed the subject and I was relieved. We never spoke of it again.

When I was ten, the family decided to take a trip to Canada for two weeks. My mother and father, grandmother and grandfather, as well as my brothers and sister all packed into our station wagon — little camper in tow — and we started off. We planned to drive up to Montreal, then across to Quebec, taking our time and staying at campgrounds near tourist spots along the way. We ended up taking a very unexpected side trip.

Somewhere along the way, my grandfather announced, "Turn right, here!" and we were off.

He directed my father to drive down highways, city streets and eventually to a home at the end of a long dirt road. The home, he declared with certainty, once belonged to his mother's sister. It could still be the home of family.

He entered the house, and sure enough the daughter of his aunt still lived there. Her own daughter lived there with her children as well.

Despite the fact that we just dropped in out of nowhere, we were asked to set up our trailer and warmly welcomed to visit for as long as we wished.

Chapter 2

I was thrilled beyond belief! Could these people be the Indians? They lived in a house. They didn't have a teepee like they showed on television. For that matter, they had a color television. That was something my cousins back home didn't even have yet. They didn't talk in one syllable words and were really nice to welcome us out of nowhere. They were not savages.

We met my grandfather's aunt. She was more than 100 years old at the time. She was sitting by a small cabin behind the main house. She explained that she preferred to live in the cabin. She was smoking a corn cob pipe, and when she saw us coming, she came running towards us with more speed than I imagined anyone that old could have mustered.

Even though she had not seen my grandfather since he was twelve years old, she went up to him, said something in words I didn't understand, hugged him and called him by his first name. She remembered him despite the fact that more than 50 years had passed!

I was amazed at how limber this woman was at her age, and how sharp her memory was. This was one really sharp lady. She was so overjoyed at seeing my grandfather again, she did a dance around him. I had to giggle because she looked so funny; such an old woman dancing like a little girl.

She looked at me and in a heavily accented voice, she said, "You're a little kittycat, you rascal, aren't you?"

WALKING THE RELINQUISHED PATH

She greeted all of us, then she and my grandfather went back to her cabin to talk. The children, myself included, were made to go play out in the yard, which we did.

Later that night, my grandmother had the job of putting me and my brothers to bed while my parents were out visiting with my grandfather's family. Just before my grandmother put out the light, she warned in a joking tone, "Better sleep with your hat on so you don't get scalped in your sleep."

My brother Tommy cringed. My older brother Jim just laughed, but I remembered thinking she was wrong. These people wouldn't hurt us. They were the most welcoming people I had ever met.

We stayed with them for a day or so more. Before we left, my sister and a girl her age who lived there exchanged addresses with the intention of writing to each other. They never did.

We drove away, never to see them again. My grandfather directed us through the maze of side streets back to the highway and we continued on with our trip. The only momentos we have of our visit are a handful of photographs of the children. My grandfather's aunt, her daughter and son-in-law didn't want to be photographed.

No one remembers any of their names, my sister lost the address long ago. The only hint of who they are is a scribble on the back of one of the photos that says, "The Hamiltons".

So deep was my grandfather's plan to cover his true family roots, that in order to visit them, he

Chapter 2

took us on a blind trip through the back roads of Canada as if it were only days, not years, since the last time he was there; but today he will not tell anyone where the house is, not even a street name so we can write them. He says over time he has forgotten.

I came back from that trip more confused than ever about what an Indian was. I was upset that during that trip I never learned the name of the tribe the people we met came from.

But I did learn that the television Indian wasn't real. They were not some evil creatures who killed white people on sight. They were wonderful people who welcomed a nephew who had been away for more than fifty years, along with his whole family, into their home without even knowing that they were coming. I know if a long lost relative, gone for more than fifty years, ever showed up at my mother's house unannounced, they would probably not be welcomed to stay.

For a short while, after our return from Canada, my grandfather was a bit more open about his Native relations. He told me stories about his life with his people and about some of the mischief he got into. Still, he was steadfast in his refusal to tell me which tribe he came from.

When I pushed him, he would tell me the words that would ring like a curse in my ears. He would say, "We turned our backs on them. What makes you think they will welcome you?"

WALKING THE RELINQUISHED PATH

I tried to point out how welcomed we were at his aunt's house. He insisted this was because we were family. He said that even though the tribe had cousins and aunts in it, they were different. They were not his mother's sister. The fact that his mother's sister was the head of that family we visited made it different. He explained, as if it was supposed to make total sense to me, "She was my mother's sister. That is why we were welcome. If they were my mother's brother's family then they would just as soon spit on us."

I asked why, but was only told the same thing over again. My grandfather insisted that if I knew what tribe his family was from and went to talk to them, they would just spit on me. I was from a family of splitters.

Only months after returning from Canada, my grandfather decided it was time to return to his silence. Perhaps my grandmother had made him stop. I don't know for sure.

It was many years before my grandfather would speak of the Indians again. That is, other than to deny he ever had any connection to them.

I walked into my adult years still wondering who the Indians were. I knew they were not savages. I knew they were not all drunkards. I knew they were not stupid. I knew that they were more than anything I could ever see on television. But who were they and why were they in my dreams?

I wondered for a long time if I would ever find my grandfather's people — my people — and if I did, would I be welcome.

Chapter 3
The Tangled Clues

To this day, as I write this chapter, my grandfather is still alive and going strong. He is, on this day, ninety-nine years old, with only two months to go until he is one hundred. He is a wonderful man who is as bright, witty and caring as any man alive, even at his advanced age. He lives with his son. Actually, to be more correct, his son needed a place to stay, so he moved into my grandfather's house. It is a good arrangement. The family feels safer knowing that someone is there in case my grandfather gets hurt.

We joke often that he will outlive all of us. And it's probably not far from the truth. He is such a strong man that last year, at the age of ninety-eight, he tripped and fell down a whole flight of cellar steps, tumbling down like a sack of potatoes and landing with a hard thump on a rock wall. His only injury was a sprained wrist.

I have noticed that my grandfather has two other unique things about him aside from his longevity and strength. He is the most adept gardener I have ever known. I have seen him grow things that should not be able to grow in this climate. Year after year, he would grow enough tomatoes to eat fresh all summer and can dozens of jars for the winter from a triangular plot of land no more than ten feet at its widest. Once, he even planted a branch of an apple tree I had broken off from another tree, and it took root and grew to another whole healthy tree!

My grandfather is like a magician when it comes to plants. It has been said, in my family, that if my grandfather planted a paper bag it would grow roses.

Another strange thing about my grandfather is that in all my life with him I have never seen him need a shave. The man has no facial hair to speak of. This made it a little hard for us kids come Christmas time, because it was popular at that time for kids to get their dads and grandfathers aftershave in cleverly shaped decanter bottles.

I was always the inquisitive child and asked him once why he never shaved. Actually, I asked him why my grandmother sometimes had more hair on her chin than he did on his.

My grandfather told me it was "one of those clues". He didn't say a clue to what. He didn't have to. He knows what I have wanted to know since I was a child. I know it was one of the clues to his heritage.

One of the most perplexing clues my grandfather gave me — he probably told this story to every child in the family over and over again, because everyone remembers it the same way — is the origin of the family name; Shaughnessy.

Chapter 3

He said that when he was twelve years old, his family came to the United States. When they were at the crossing, they had to pass through customs and immigration. It was 1914, a time when a lot of Irish people were coming to America.

When it was his father's turn at immigration, he was asked what the family name was. His father declared, "We have no family name. We are Shawwanashee Indians." So the customs official, who had already written so many Irish names that day, just wrote "Shaughnessy" on the paperwork.

My grandfather said they were so happy to be thought of as Irish that his father said nothing to correct it.

This is a great story, but probably not the truth. Still, I took it for fact, because of my grandfather's consistent telling of it. But no matter how hard I searched, I could not find any trace of a Shawwanashee Indian tribe. There were Shawnee, but it only came close.

When I asked my grandfather if the tribe were Shawnee he said, "No, that's not it," but didn't offer to correct me.

I tried to look up my grandfather's blood line at the time, but since it was before the Internet was full of genealogical sites, and he was born in another country, getting actual paperwork would have to wait. For now, I could only rely on what he told me. That wasn't much.

He told me his father was named Fred, just like himself. His mother was named Delima. I met her as a child, but she was in a nursing home with very little understanding of what was going on around her.

When I was a small child, every week, my grandfather would take me to visit her. She always thought I was her youngest daughter, Mary, or my grandfather's daughter. She never could recall, from moment to moment, which of her sons my grandfather was.

In my search, I visited the nursing home where she passed away, they had record of her being there for many years, but had no records of her parents. So I was stuck, because my grandfather wouldn't go back beyond that, once again using the excuse that he didn't remember.

Some time later, my grandfather's sister, June, started to talk about things that didn't make any sense. She was always the "black sheep" of the family and had many problems as a young woman that caused some in the family to believe she wasn't completely sane.

She was a sweet old woman who lived alone in an apartment facility for the aged. My grandfather and she were not really close, but my mother would take her shopping from time to time. When she did, I would occasionally tag along.

My great aunt June never wanted to talk about Indians. She, like all my grandfather's siblings, felt that if my grandfather wanted me to know more about our family secret, he would tell me himself.

She had one son, my great-cousin Jim. Jim lives in California with his own children.

Chapter 3

Toward the end of my Aunt June's life, she began to tell Jim stories about Indians and other family secrets. But since my aunt June was not very well at the time, and she seemed to be slipping into senility, he really didn't listen much. She seemed to talk nonsense at times about having a different last name and not being what she said she was. She wanted her son to know who the family was before she died.

Unfortunately, she couldn't explain herself well enough for Jim to understand, and no one else took her very seriously.

When she passed away, we discovered that she left behind some papers including copies of her baptism certificate, her immigration papers and her citizenship papers. These papers were very old and had her maiden name, Shaughnessy, on them.

But oddly enough, she crossed out the name Shaughnessy on each of these documents and scrawled in the name Chatigney. It was obvious it was done at a much later date as the handwriting showed a shaky, frail hand.

Where did the name Chatigney come from? There were no Chatigney's in our family that anyone knew of. She even went so far as to purchase her own headstone with the name Chatigney carved on it.

On her baptism certificate she changed her father's last name to Chatigney as well. She left a note telling her son that Chatigney was the family's original name.

Could this be a clue?

WALKING THE RELINQUISHED PATH

I can't begin to tell you how much of a ruckus this caused in the family. My grandfather and the few siblings who outlived their sister, June, insisted she was nuts. There was no Chatigney ever in the family and they didn't know where she got that name.

But her son, Jim, insisted that he remembered her telling him once that Chatigney was their "real Indian name" before they were named Shaughnessy. He also remembered her saying that she knew they spelled it different, but she couldn't remember how they spelled it, so she spelled it the best she could.

Hearing Jim's story about his mother gave me new hope that I might be able to find something on the family now that I had copies of her baptism and immigration papers. At least I found the names of my grandfather's grandparents. But the question was, were they Shaughnessys or Chatigneys? And how was I going to find out? I was not in a position to be able to afford a trip up north to check out the city and town hall records. Canada is a big place and I didn't even have a city name to start with.

My grandfather told stories of being born in North Bay, Ontario. He told stories of how he lived just down the road from the famous Dion quintuplets. That was someplace to start. If this story was true, it would mean that his family would be on record as living there. There should be some birth records of him or his siblings in that town.

I called the City Hall of North Bay. They had no records of any child named Fred Shaughnessy

Chapter 3

being born there in 1902 or the year before or after. They had no records of a baby surnamed Shaughnessy being born in 1902 at all. The woman was very helpful and even checked the tax records for that year. There was no record of any Shaughnessy paying taxes that year. She checked for Chatigney, using the most common spelling she could and did not find anything in the town records either.

She told me she would check a few more places, so I should call her back in a few days. When I called back she told me there was a record of a Fred Shaughnessy and his family living in North bay starting in 1909. There was no record of where they came from, or any other reference to them. So she couldn't say where they moved after they left. There was no record of a Fred Chatigney and family at all.

So, I knew my grandfather did live in North Bay for at least 2 years. But why would he insist he was born there?

Could it be that my grandfather simply didn't remember? After all, he spent so many years making up stories to cover up his heritage that I had to wonder if he lost the truth along the way.

I spent many weeks writing letters to different city and town halls in Canada, trying to locate the true place my grandfather was born. I tried to remember the names of the people we visited on our trip to Canada when I was a child. The only thing I knew was that the house was in or around Penetanguishene, and the family name —

according to the scrawling on the back of an old photograph — was Hamilton.

I first went to several libraries but could not find a phone book for Penetanguishene.

A quick look at Ontario's section of the Canada 411 website revealed a maximum return of 500 Hamiltons in that province.

There were fewer when the search was limited to Penetanguishene only, but they were not the correct people. So this was a dead-end. Besides, I wasn't totally sure the house was in Penetanguishene proper. It really seemed to be out in the backwoods, and Penetanguishene was a rather modern city, even back then.

I wrote a detailed letter to the city hall of Penetanguishene. I was careful to enclose a return envelope with correct postage, and even told them to call collect if they had any questions or would like to talk to me. Still, I never received an answer. Maybe, like North Bay, Penetanguishene was a wild goose chase.

It was just about this time that I felt like I hit a brick wall. I had sent letters out to every city or town office that I had ever heard any of my relatives mention, only to hear nothing in return. The few that did reply were dead-ends. The best were nice letters telling me they looked but didn't find anything and wishing me luck. The worst were printed letters informing me of how I could, for a price, hire someone to go through their records for me.

Chapter 3

I wrote to several churches as well. None of whom wrote back at all.

With frustration as a motivator, I began to make phone calls to any place where I sent information. That is, if I could find their phone number to start with. I was shocked how many phones just rang and rang, never being answered. It got so that I began to wonder if there was anyone really up there in Canada.

When someone did answer, I was usually told that they had not seen any information from me, and was asked to once again send all the information I had sent originally. Which I did. Still, nothing ever came back to me.

I finally felt like I was driving my head into a brick wall. I decided to give up the search. It was filling my life with frustration, and costing me more money than I could afford just in phone calls, photocopies and postage!

I resolved to put it all away. "I don't need to know what tribe we are from anyway," I would tell myself. After all, my grandfather was probably right. Even if I found them, they wouldn't want anything to do with me. My family left them long ago. We took off when things were getting rough. We were splitters!

Chapter 4
Uncle Bob's Mystery

Just about the time I decided that I had taken all I could of dead-end leads and endless international phone calls for nothing, the most amazing thing happened.

I was dreaming a very unusual dream. I dreamed that I was the rain. I had never dreamt anything like that before. How could I be the rain? It is impossible to explain exactly how I felt, being the rain. But the best I can say is that it didn't feel like anything I had ever experienced before. I was the rain and I was gently falling down on a huge oak tree, dripping off its long branches and absorbing into the ground below it. The roots of the tree then drew me up into them. I felt warm and wonderful as I was drawn up into the trunk of the tree via the roots. Then I was pushed into each and every leaf as it opened to the sky. The sun shined down on the leaves and I was evaporated into the air. Soon I was flying and I came to stop in an endless, clear, blue sky. I was no longer water. I was now myself.

In front of me stood an old man. He had gray and white hair. His face was worn and weathered. He wore a white animal fur around his

Chapter 4

shoulders. The fur appeared to be as old as he was. He was holding a stick or a pike of some kind that had feathers tied to it. He had a pouch in front of him that looked like it was made from a beaver's tail. As I looked at him with amazement, he seemed to get even older and more frail in front of my eyes.

He said, "When I die, it is gone. Find me before I die."

Like a flash, the dream ended and I was in bed. I didn't get back to sleep for the rest of the night. I wondered who this man was, if in fact he wasn't just a figment of my imagination. It was almost unthinkable to even consider he could be real and that somehow he tried to reach to me with this dream.

How could it be? I finally concluded that the dream must be my subconscious' way of telling me I could not give up, dead-ends or not.

Still, even if I could convince myself that the dream was just a figment of my imagination, I couldn't shake the intense feeling of panic it caused to even think about it. I felt like I had a deadline now.

Frankly, the feeling of having a deadline made me feel a bit bitter about all the dead-ends I was hitting. I felt like shouting back to the feeling and whatever was behind it, whether real or imagined, "If you want me to do this, open some doors for me!" Actually, I probably did yell it out loud more than once; probably a lot more than once.

As if a cruel answer to my frustrated prayer, my mother's cousin Bob died.

WALKING THE RELINQUISHED PATH

To backtrack a little, my mother's cousin Bob was always known to me as my Uncle Bob. His father and my grandfather were brothers, which really made him my second cousin, or great-cousin depending on who you asked. But since he was so much older than I was, he was considered an Uncle to me and my siblings. When I was growing up, he and his family would visit from time to time.

He and his wife, Ruth, were rather close to my Mother and Father at different times in their lives. They use to square dance together.

Since, as a teen, I square danced as well, it was usually at dances that I saw my Uncle Bob. I had no idea he led a clandestine life. I didn't know, and no one bothered to tell me, that he had made the connection and was living the family secret.

All the while, as I struggled to find out who my family were, he attended powwows and socials. He studied the customs and language. He even headed a local Indian social organization in his hometown. Despite all the questioning and prying I did, no one ever breathed a word of it to me. Not one word!

The way I found out was rather sad. I had gone to visit my mother some weeks after my Uncle Bob passed away. That afternoon, his widow, Ruth, decided to drop in for a visit with my mother. The mood was somber, but she was past the worst of her grief and starting to be able to make light of things.

As we were sitting having tea, my mother asked Ruth how she was holding out and if she needed any help. Ruth said that she was doing well

Chapter 4

and that she was on top of things. She bragged that she even cleaned out the closet of her husbands things.

My mother mentioned that it must have been a hard thing to do.

Ruth said, "No. Not really. I was so glad to get rid of all that stupid Indian crap. Finally no more 'redskin's buckskins' in my house," she said *redskin's buckskins* with a thick, blunt television Indian accent.

I didn't understand what I was hearing. What did she mean?

My mother asked if he had that much Indian stuff and suggested she could have sold it rather than toss it away.

Ruth answered her suggestion by bragging that now that Bob had gone to the "happy hunting ground" she couldn't wait to get rid of all the Indian nonsense. She went on to say it wasn't worth selling. If she advertised she had it to sell, people would know she had it to start with.

My mother agreed, and then went on to talk about something else.

I broke in and asked, "Aunt Ruth, are you saying Uncle Bob had all kinds of Indian stuff?"

She said, "Sure. My bedroom closet was like a damned wigwam! He was crazy about that stuff. Always wanted me and the kids to like it, too. It was all crazy stuff if you ask me."

"Did he know what tribe we were?" I asked with intense anticipation?

Walking the Relinquished Path

"I don't know. It's written down somewhere at the house. Call me and I'll let you know," she turned to my mother and they talked about something else.

Several more times I tried to bring up the subject that afternoon, but it was clear no one but me wanted to talk about it.

The next day I phoned Aunt Ruth and asked her if she had found the tribal name yet. She told me she didn't have the time to look. I pushed further, but she was determined not to bother.

I asked her if she had any of my Uncle Bob's personal effects that I could look through. I also asked that if she found any Indian things he had, could she give them or even sell them to me, rather than throw them away.

She promised she would call me if she found anything more.

I called her every few days for several months. Each time she told me she had nothing.

Finally, she told me in no uncertain terms that she thought all the "damned Indian bullshit" was over when her husband died and that I was not to call her ever again about it. I begged her not to be angry and tried to explain what this meant to me.

She said, "Tell someone who cares!"

In frustration I asked, "Who would care anyway?"

As if struck by the lightning of kindness, she surprised me by answering my rhetorical question. She answered, "Bob had a step brother. His name is

Chapter 4

Josh. Call him, he might care." Then she gave me the phone number.

I was momentarily stunned, then I snapped to my senses, thanked her, and quickly called the number she gave me.

Josh answered the phone and I introduced myself to him. At first he seemed annoyed, as if he was expecting me to try and sell him something. His whole tone and manner changed when I told him why I was calling.

"Bob," he said, "was really into his Indian background. Ever since we were kids. Before his father died, he gave Bob some Indian stuff that use to be his. He was hooked after that."

"What did he give him?" I asked, hoping to hear something like, 'official tribal paperwork.'

"He gave him some photos and some old bird wings or something," Josh answered. "It was a long time ago. We were only kids, you know. I don't remember anymore." He hemmed and hawed a little bit then said something about having to go cut the grass in his yard. Considering it was late fall at the time, I knew he just wanted to get rid of me.

"Do you know what tribe he was from?" I asked, ignoring his comment about the grass. I really didn't expect him to know, but I had to ask.

"Sure," he said with confidence. "He was Mohawk. I remember when we went up to the Mohawk Reserve in Canada to get him in the tribe."

"What reserve? What happened?" I was on the edge of my seat. I grabbed a pen and pad of

WALKING THE RELINQUISHED PATH

paper to write down what he told me. This is what he said:

Bob's whole focus in his young life was to be recognized by the tribe. He loved the idea that he was an Indian. He felt a strong urge to discover and live by his traditional roots as much as he could. He was, as Josh put it, so obsessed he ate, drank and slept thinking about who he was. When Josh and his brother Bob were young men in their late teens, Bob had collected a pile of paperwork he insisted he had to bring to the Mohawk Indian's in Canada so he could be recognized.

Josh had just purchased his first car and they decided it was time for a road trip. One morning, paperwork in hand, they jumped into the car and Josh drove all day and part of the night until they came to the Mohawk reserve in Canada.

They camped out on the road, sleeping in the car that night. Bright and early the next day they entered the reserve. They went to the Tribal office and were taken to a room where a very pretty young woman was working behind the desk.

Bob gave her the paperwork that he had. She was gone awhile, but then came back with a big, old book. In the book she found some names and started to write them down on another piece of paper. He said Bob was almost jumping out of his skin as she copied the names from the book onto this paper.

Bob asked, "It's true then. They are there? I'm related?"

Chapter 4

The woman, who Josh emphasized was just about the most beautiful woman he had ever seen, walked over with a big smile to hand Bob the paper. At that point, Josh turned to the woman and said, "Miss, you are one beautiful squaw!" He had no idea that he was calling her a whore.

She looked at him with the most disgusted expression, then shouted at the top of her lungs. Immediately, three big guys came running in to see what was wrong. She said something about him and his brother being insulting jerks and the three men asked them to leave.

He said at the time he didn't know what he did wrong. He also said that Bob pleaded for her to give him the paper before he went. She replied, "Not on your life. Come back when you have learned some respect!"

He said he was more than happy to leave, but Bob lingered and begged. He tried to explain that his brother didn't know what he was saying. Finally, the three Mohawk men forced them to leave.

Bob didn't talk to Josh all the drive home, except to curse and swear at him for destroying his life.

What a story. But was it true? I made Josh swear on his mother's grave that what he told me was the total truth. He said it was.

I asked him if he was sure the tribe was Mohawk. He said he was positive. He couldn't remember the name of the place, but he said it was the reserve where there had been some trouble with the government not long ago. He remembered that distinctly because he recalled watching the conflict on the news and telling his wife that it was the place he had visited with his brother.

I asked if Bob left his paperwork there? He said he wasn't sure. But he said that Bob was able to get back in touch with them later. He told me he was an accepted member of the tribe and even carried an ID card which he used to join a local Indian organization in his home town. He had no idea what the name of the organization was.

I thanked him, and he promised that if he remembered anymore he would call me back.

I hung up the phone then started for the bathroom for a much needed break, but stopped dead in my tracks. Did I really know what tribe we were? Were we Mohawk? Could it be true that Uncle Bob had been a card carrying Mohawk tribal member?

The next morning, I started my hunt for the Indian organization in the town where my Uncle Bob lived. After sorting out the few Indian organizations for people from India, I found that I was left with one place. It was a local Indian Social club. The library had a listing for them in an old book of town organizations, but nothing for many years.

I called the number listed. A woman with an old and frail sounding voice answered. She told me that she had not worked for them for many years. She said, "I don't know if that place is there

Chapter 4

anymore. I don't think they ever rebuilt after the fire."

I asked her if she could direct me to anyone who might know. She gave me the name and phone number of a man named John Little Bird.

I called the number and a man answered. "Is this John Little Bird?" I asked.

"Huh," the man seemed a bit stunned. "Yes. Yes it is," he said after an uncomfortable pause. "Sorry if I sound surprised. No one has called me that in years. Most people call me Smithy." He laughed. "What can I do for you."

I explained to him that I was related to Bob Shaughnessy and asked him if he remembered Bob. He did. Actually he was a good friend of Bob's and was even at the funeral! This was great.

I asked him what he knew about Bob's roots and tribal connections, and explained to him what Josh told me. He agreed with Josh that Bob was a Mohawk. He said Bob had been the head of the lodge for several years.

He talked about how Bob was such a great guy and how much he missed him. He went on and on about how much Bob loved his culture and how he even made all his own regalia. "Nothing store bought was traditional enough for Bob," he laughed.

"You are sure Bob was Mohawk?" I asked.

"Yes. He was listed on the records as being Mohawk. He wouldn't be listed as Mohawk if he were Navajo," he said.

"Would he have to show any proof that he was really Mohawk to get into the lodge? Could someone off the street come in and say, I'm a Mohawk without proof and get a membership in the lodge?" I dared to ask.

"No way," he said firmly. "You had to have something to prove who you were. In the beginning, when the lodge first opened, people use to join saying they were Indians, then they would break things up and cause trouble. They really hated us back then. We even moved the lodge several times because they would break all our windows, even on our cars!" he explained. "Later, we had to make sure because some people would say they were Indians to get in because they thought we had some big secret we were hiding and they wanted to be in on it. But mostly, we had to check because we needed the security. You know how many times thugs tried to burn our lodge down?"

"What a horrible thing. But good for my cause," I thought. After all, this meant Uncle Bob had produced proof he was a Mohawk Indian. If he had it, I could find it, too.

I asked if I could get copies of the records the lodge had on my Uncle Bob. I explained how important this was to me. If I could show Bob was a member of the tribe, it would be easy to show a direct blood link to Bob. I would know who I was, and maybe even find my people.

He promised he would help me as much as he could, but that might be limited. The lodge had been burned down about ten years before, and the only records left were in his basement. He said he would look through them and find anything he

Chapter 4

could. He asked me if I could call him back in a week.

Finally, I asked him if he knew which reserve Bob was affiliated with. He said he didn't have any memory of that, but that it would be on the records.

That week was one of the longest weeks of my life. I filled the time doing research trying to find out which Mohawk reserve in Canada had a conflict with the Canadian government in recent years.

My husband, Paul, believed the reserve I was looking for was Kanehsatake. He recalled a big conflict there in or about 1990.

He was probably right, but I didn't want to contact the tribal office there until I had something concrete from Uncle Bob's old lodge.

I called John Little Bird a week after we first spoke. He had nothing but bad news for me. He said Bob's records were not among the few he had saved from the rubble left of the lodge after the last fire. He was sorry but he couldn't help me.

I asked him if there was anything else he remembered about Bob's tribal connections. He said, "Nope. Nothing except he was Sioux."

"Sioux?" I said with surprise. "You mean Mohawk." I corrected.

"No, he was Sioux," he answered.

"You said Mohawk before. His brother said Mohawk. Are you sure he wasn't Mohawk?" I pushed.

WALKING THE RELINQUISHED PATH

"You know, he could be Mohawk," John said uneasily. "I don't remember. I'm Sioux, you see. So everyone is Sioux to me," he laughed.

"Yeah, he was probably Mohawk," he continued. "I can't remember. If I told you Mohawk last time we talked, then he was probably Mohawk. I can't remember. I'm sorry but you're asking me to think way back." He apologized again, then assured me if he remembered anything else or found any paperwork he would call me. He never did.

So, what could I do? The only lead I had was to contact Kanehsatake and tell them my story. If they could find a Bob Shaughnessy on their rolls, then I could take it from there. If they couldn't find him, my grandfather or his parents on the roll, I was stuck again.

My hands were shaking as I dialed the number to Kanehsatake's office. Each ring of the phone seemed like it was years long. My fear grew by the second. Finally, a woman answered the phone.

I told her all about what was going on. I told her my Uncle Bob's story about going up there to get paperwork and how he almost had the paper in his hand. She asked if I knew what book the names were in, or what those names were. I had no clue.

I told her how they were chased away and how later he got the paperwork, because he used that paperwork to prove his tribal connection when he was admitted as a member of the lodge in his town. I also told her how his lodge records had been

Chapter 4

destroyed in a fire and how his wife tossed out everything else.

Admittedly, I was giving her little to go on. If Bob was on the list, it would be easy enough. If he wasn't, it was a shot in the dark.

After speaking on the phone, I got all my paperwork together and sent it to the reservation. It took me a few days longer than I expected to get everything in order.

After a few weeks of not hearing anything, I called Kanehsatake and spoke to the woman again. She told me that things had gotten rather busy there since I mailed my stuff and that she would get to it when she could.

Several weeks later I called again. She said she was just about to write me to tell me that not one name from the list I sent her was on the rolls, now or in the past. She had spoken to the woman who worked there at the time Bob and his brother claimed to have gone to the office. She was sure if anything like that had really happened the woman would still remember it, but she didn't. So it was her opinion that the story about how Bob and his brother went to the Reservation was a family myth.

She also told me she talked to a few other offices on my behalf and found nothing there either. "I don't know what you are. But you are not Mohawk," she said with confidence, then hung up the phone.

I was shocked. What would I do now? That is, what would I do after I stopped crying?

WALKING THE RELINQUISHED PATH

I had only one place to go. I went to my grandfather's house.

"Pipere," I said. "Bob Shaughnessy had proof of what tribe we are."

"How did he get that?" he asked me with surprise.

"I don't know. I think your brother gave it to him," I answered.

"So, what did he tell you?" My grandfather asked. "Did he tell you before he died?"

"No. But his step brother Josh said he was Mohawk and the man who use to run the lodge here in town said he thinks he was Mohawk, but the records were destroyed in a fire. Josh said that your people came from Kanehsatake in Canada."

"He's wrong," my grandfather said flatly. "We aren't Mohawk."

"If not, what were we?" I asked. I'm sure I almost whined out the question.

"None of your business," he said.

"But if you won't tell me, how do I know that we are not really Mohawk and you are just not telling me that?" I dared.

"We are not Mohawk," my grandfather said firmly.

I walked away, not quite sure I believed him.

My Uncle Bob had left me with quite a mystery. It seemed the more I looked, the more questions I found. Answers were few and far between.

So now I had two questions mucking up the waters of my search. The first; was the family name

Chapter 4

Shaughnessy or Chatigney? The second; were we Mohawk or was that just Josh's bad memory; or perhaps a lie he made up to get me off his back?

Would I ever find what my Uncle Bob cherished so much? I often wonder how he felt, alone in his belief that being what he truly was, an Indian, was important. I wonder if we had learned about each other's desire before he passed away, if it would have made as big a difference in his life as I know it would have made in mine.

Chapter 5
My Not So Cunning Plan

I devised a plan in hopes of tricking my grandfather into telling me what I needed to know.

I heard once that people of Indian blood could go to Harvard University for free. I wasn't sure if it were totally true, but if I heard about it, perhaps my grandfather had, too.

Now, I had no intention of going to Harvard. I never had any intention of gaining Indian status for any monetary reason whatsoever. Still, I thought the idea might present my grandfather with incentive to give me the information I needed.

The first step was to speak with my mother about it. I had to convince her that it was possible that if my grandfather allowed me to make the connection to my tribal roots, then I would be able to go to college for free. But I didn't feel good about lying to my elders, so I called Harvard and was told that it was true. Native American Fellowships are awarded annually on a competitive basis of merit and financial need to American Indian students who are planning a career in American Indian affairs. I would be stretching the truth a bit, but I wouldn't be outright lying. The program existed, but I knew that

Chapter 5

even if I had tribal recognition, I would likely not qualify for it. Not to mention, I had no intention of pursuing such a program.

Regardless, I told my mother what I found out. We talked about how great it would be for me, even at my age, to go back to college; and to go to Harvard no less. My mother thought it was a great idea. She suggested I come over some time when my grandfather was visiting with her and she would help me pitch the idea.

The next time I knew my grandfather was going to be at my mother's house, I visited. I figured my mother would jump on the bandwagon and help me with my mild deception. She did, though she didn't know my plan.

We both told my grandfather about the Harvard fellowship. My mother went on and on about how expensive Harvard was and how wonderful it would be if I could go there for free.

I talked about how great it would be to attend such a prestigious school. My mother bragged that she would be so proud to have a Harvard graduate in the family.

My grandfather said he heard that Indians sometimes went to school for free if their grades were good. I reminded him of my Dean's List status in college. He thought for a few moments, then after some more coaxing, he finally said, "Look at the tribes around the Huron."

"The Huron?" I asked. "Do you mean the Huron people or Lake Huron?"

WALKING THE RELINQUISHED PATH

"There were a lot of Hurons running around then," he said, as if he really didn't want to answer. "Maybe they were Huron. Maybe they were Cree. I don't know," he said.

"You do to, Pa," my mother said sternly. "Just tell her so she can go to school for free, will ya. She's not going to go running up there looking for them. She just wants to go to school!"

"Yeah, yeah." My grandfather turned to look at me. "You think so," he said to my mother while starring into my eyes. "But I know what she's up to."

"Me?" I said innocently. "I'm not up to anything, Pipere. I just feel if admitting my heritage will help me get ahead in life, you owe it to me to tell me."

"I don't owe you anything," he said with a laugh. "Children owe their Elders not Elders owe their children."

His statement was almost as good as a clue. I had read up on several tribes and about their traditional attitude towards their children. Many tribes, such as the Pennacook, were very free ranging parents with their children. They believed that their children were gifts to them and they would go so far as not to reprimand them for wrong doing. They believed, I read, that since their children were gifts to them, it was their job to keep their children cared for and happy all their lives. Soon enough, they would grow up and have to face the harshness of adulthood. According to the books I read, even into adulthood, parents felt obligated to their

Chapter 5

children and would sacrifice their own comfort and happiness for their offspring long after those offspring were grown and had children of their own.

I read that other tribes, such as the Ojibwa, had a more utilitarian view of children. Though they loved and cherished them just as much as the Pennacook did, they did not believe in letting the children run their parent's lives. Children had a working place in society. They were not always free to do as they wished, and they were reprimanded when they did wrong. But the most notable difference was that — based on my reading, as I have never talked to a traditional Ojibwa parent about this — they believed that it was a child's duty to help their parents when they were old. Children were expected to care for their elderly parents to the same extent that they were cared for by their parents. It was more than expected, it was required.

Could my grandfather's words be a clue that he grew up with the philosophy of a tribe like the Ojibwa? Was I reading too much into his statement? I remembered back to when his wife, my grandmother, was dying. My mother worked day and night to care for her. My dear mother was so worn out after months of intense twenty-four hour care, she asked my grandfather to allow her to let the hospice center send in daily assistance to take some of the pressure off of my mother. My grandfather's answer was blunt and clear. "I will not have a stranger taking care of your mother on her deathbed. We had you children so we would have someone to take care of us when this time comes!"

WALKING THE RELINQUISHED PATH

Could this have been a reflection of a social value he was taught as a child?

My grandfather said nothing more about the Harvard fellowship for the rest of the afternoon. If I brought it up, he pretended that his hearing aid wasn't working and would just say, "What? What are you saying?" until I stopped asking.

Finally, when I was getting up to go home, he said. "Look at the Huron people. You might find the Lamoureauxs there."

I rushed home and turned on my computer to find out anything I could about the Hurons. The first thing I found was that they were not really named Hurons. That was a name given to them by the French. They were really called Wyandot. Why didn't my grandfather call them by their correct name?

I made a list of the different Huron tribal offices I could find. Unfortunately, all who had any Internet sites were in the United States. I was really more interested in contacting the Canadian Wyandot. It looked like the Internet was going to be a waste of time. I had to go back to making international phone calls and writing letters.

Figuring that if I could narrow my search down a bit it would help my phone bill, I called my grandfather.

"Pipere, can you tell me what Wyandot reservation your family was connected to?" I asked.

"What are you talking about?"

Chapter 5

"You told me to look at the Huron people," I reminded. "So what Wyandot reservation should I start with?"

"I said Huron, not Wayinwhatever," he snapped back.

"Pipere, the Wyandot are the Huron," I said, not knowing what he was up to.

"Oh, yeah that's right," he laughed. "I guess you caught me and figured out my lie."

"Lie?"

"Yeah. We weren't Huron. I just said that to keep you busy," he explained in a playful tone that made me angry.

"Why. Why won't you tell me the truth?" I begged.

"Like Harvard was the truth?" he said.

It was obvious he knew all along that I had no intention of going to Harvard and it was a rouse to get him to spill the beans. "Well, not really. They do have a program, but I have nothing to do with it."

"And I don't know nothing about any Indians!" he said firmly, then hung up the phone.

For a long, bone-silent moment, I stood there holding the phone to my ear, feeling like the rug had just been pulled out from under me.

Not only had I got caught in a lie to my grandfather, but once again I was given a tribal name only to be told it was made up.

Then it struck me. What if my grandfather was lying about lying? What if he changed his mind about telling me the tribal name and now was lying

WALKING THE RELINQUISHED PATH

to cover up what he said before? What if we were Huron? It was possible, I figured.

Right away, I returned to my computer and contacted the few websites I found run by Wyandot people. I got on a mailing list run by a very nice Wyandot man and posted my family information there. Nothing helpful happened.

I mailed my information to several Wyandot offices. Most were very nice to me, but none could find any hint of our family line in their rolls. One person I spoke to on the phone was very nice to me the first time I talked to him. But after I sent him my information, and he failed to find any of the names I gave him on a tribal roll, his whole attitude changed. He accused me of being a "wannabe" Indian who was trying to steal his culture.

I got off the phone so upset I cried. How could someone say such a thing. Why would anyone want to steal anyone else's culture?

Chapter 6
What's In a Name

Shakespeare once said the immortal words, "What's in a name? A rose by any other name would smell as sweet." It is the truth, but if roses were named stink weed or hog's perfume, would they be such a popular gift to give the one you love? I think not.

A name is an important thing. I have seen television shows that suggest that the name you get as a child can mold the whole way you look at the world as you grow up. It definitely molds the way others look at you. As a parent I know that young children today who have old-fashioned names, which were totally acceptable just forty years ago, such as Hildergard or Ethel, will be teased and rejected by their peers. This can have a terrible effect on their emotional well being.

It seems it is difficult for us to separate our persona and our name. Our names are our identity. A name represents us, and in many ways may even create us. Not having a name is something that is inconceivable. Many of us have our names chosen for us even before we are born. We name our pets, the things we own, some of us even name our body parts! Names are very important to us because with a name, we attach the concept of personality and life.

Not to have a name would not just rob us of a label, but would imply we have no personality; no reason for existence. Likewise, our surname gives us a sense of identity.

America has often been called the great melting pot. This is a wonderful concept for the most part. People come to the United States from different places and they become Americans. They change their allegiance from their place of birth to the United States. But because of the great freedoms we have, today no one is forced to change their total way of life. They are free to live, eat, worship and even talk the way they wish and still be welcome, turning the melting pot concept into more of a rich stew pot of different chunks of cultures put together to make a whole.

This is not the way it always was. When my grandfather's family came to the United States they were forced to give up everything that identified them as a people in order to live quietly without being the target of prejudice and hatred.

My family could not understand why it was so important for me to connect to my heritage. Once my father asked me, "Why aren't you looking for your LaVigne roots? Why aren't you trying to connect with your French ancestors?"

It was a really good question. What was it about my grandfather's roots that meant so much more to me than the roots on my European side?

Chapter 6

Was it that my grandfather's past represented a forbidden fruit of sorts? Could it just be the need to have something you know is being denied you?

I searched my soul, but didn't find this was the case. Even though I did believe I would find enjoyment in showing my family some kind of positive proof of exactly who we were, it was not the focus of what I was feeling. My feelings went much further back; back to the time when I was a small child and my grandfather took me for walks in the woods; back to the dreams I had been having all my life about the people I visited on the back of the giant white horse; back to a gut-wretching feeling I experienced whenever I thought about this seemingly endless search of mine.

I didn't want to know just because it was something denied me. I wanted to know because it was something inside me. It was something that could not be denied to me, because I was born with it.

But knowing it was there just wasn't enough. I, like any other person, needed to put a label on it. What exactly was this part of me. Was I Mohawk? Was I something else? There were so many tribes living in the area where my grandfather claimed to be born. They were often displaced by settlers, wars and other pressures. Because of this, at any given time, just about any tribe could have resided in the area where my grandfather hailed from. Looking at maps and geographical data was getting me nowhere.

WALKING THE RELINQUISHED PATH

Nevertheless, I began to learn what I could about the different Indians in the region. I hoped that something in their stories would trigger a memory of the long forgotten tales my grandfather told me when I was a child. It didn't help.

What I came away with was the understanding that even in a relatively small region like the area around the Great Lakes, there were so many tribes. Some shared a common root language, some shared common ways of life and even stories, but for the most part they were different. They each had their own history, and most importantly, their own perspective of the world.

I couldn't possibly hope to understand my people by trying to understand all Indians as a collective group. I had to know the individual and unique people.

About this time in my life, I was working for a small magazine that published mostly new-aged themed stories. Everything from Atlantis to psychic healings were covered in the magazine. The owners of the magazine were very much into whatever was the new-aged fad of the day and they focused the publication in that direction.

All at once, they started to publish stories about Native Spirituality, using native symbols and words to defend and promote their new-age religious views. I called the owner about this, protesting that it was disrespectful of them to publish such things. Besides, it was just plain wrong as far as the facts go. Medicine wheels did not represent the signs of the zodiac, not all Indians

Chapter 6

believe they are the lost tribe of Israel, and most importantly, Indian peoples were individual clans with their own belief systems. It was just flat out wrong to publish a story that said all Indians believe any one thing. It was simply not true.

The owners did not take my concerns seriously. Despite my concerns, the issue ran and was well received by its audience.

Several more issues of the publication followed; each one with more and more new-age rhetoric disguised as Native American Indian culture and belief.

I began to understand what the Wyandot man on the phone was angry about. Here I was, only a quarter Indian blood, not knowing what tribe or culture I truly hailed from, and I was becoming infuriated with these articles.

Every sentence I read that started with the words, "All Native Americans believe," made me wince. Every time I read about how eagles represent the power of rose quartz crystals and celtic crosses, I wanted to scream.

Please don't misunderstand. It is not that I have any negative opinions about the new-aged religion or new-aged spirituality, it is simply not the same as Indian spirituality. They may have much in common, especially if you only look on the surface, but they are not the same. You don't do a Sun Dance to fix your karma. You don't smudge with sweetgrass to focus your Chi. And most of all, you don't tell people you are Indian so you can make them pay you to teach them how to Sun Dance or smudge with sweetgrass.

I looked at what the owners were doing. I looked around at others like them and realized why the Wyandot man yelled at me, accusing me of trying to steal his culture. Stealing his culture was exactly what these people around me were doing.

I couldn't continue to sit there and quietly watch these people while they imitated the beliefs of native cultures, purposely giving them different meanings. For the most part, it seemed to me that they didn't even care what the truth really was. I cringed when people at the magazine started signing their articles with monikers like Golden Hawk, Morning Sun and Rolling Thunder added to their real names.

One day I was talking with another employee who had just attended one of these new-aged Indian gathering conferences. I was excited at first to hear what she had to say about what happened, but before long I was sad and upset. Still, she was excited and overjoyed with her experience.

The man running the conference said he was a Blackfoot Indian. He claimed to be the holder of some sacred symbol of great medicine. He also claimed to be a Chief of his tribe, but I never found any proof that he was even a tribal member, never mind a Chief.

She said when they arrived, they checked in, paid their money and entered the center where the ceremony was going to take place. The ceremony itself was Hopi in origin. I guess she didn't think

Chapter 6

there was anything strange about a Blackfoot performing a Hopi ceremony.

She said that she learned a lot at the conference. These facts included learning that her Greek zodiac sign — capricorn — was represented by the bear on the Indian zodiac medicine wheel, and that her spirit element was rose quartz because of the 'moon' she was born under.

I didn't know if I was going to laugh or choke as she talked about how they made a meditation circle and chanted Sioux "words of power" to bring their chakra energy in focus.

I had to ask her why he wasn't using Blackfoot words if the man doing the ceremony was indeed Blackfoot. She said that he chose words that were the most powerful and which healed the Karma and Kundalini power of the soul.

I wish I was able to say that I couldn't believe my ears, but after months of working on the magazine stories, I knew what she was saying was what really happened. What was worse, she believed every word of it was an authentic representation of the beliefs of all Native peoples.

"Did the Sioux really have words that would heal Karma and Kundalini?" I dared ask. "I mean, I don't think the Sioux and the Hindus hung out together."

"You don't get it," she replied.

"Explain it to me," I said with defiance.

"Well, Hindus and Native Americans have a lot of beliefs in common," she explained. "That's why you can use Sioux words to heal your Karma.

WALKING THE RELINQUISHED PATH

Did you know that you can use a sweat lodge to find out what kind of Indian you were in a past life?" she added.

"Who said you were an Indian in a past life?" I asked.

"I must be, or I wouldn't feel so welcome in these ceremonies," she answered.

"Well, I guess I'm just an Indian in this life," I said. "I think I would have been very uncomfortable at that ceremony."

"You say so. But if you had the money to come, you would have loved it. The energy was so wonderful. Everyone was resonating with the frequency of the eagle," she said as if I should be impressed. "We were all our inner Native American selves," she said. "By the way," she added, "they don't like to be called Indians. They are not from India."

"But you said they do have Karma," I snickered.

She huffed and walked away. As I watched her leave, I realized that no matter what I said, it would never occur to her to even ask why a man who claimed to be a Blackfoot Chief would be doing a Hopi ceremony rather than a Blackfoot one. She would never give a second thought as to why a Lakota medicine wheel should have anything to do with the Greek zodiac. She would never think there was anything strange about the fact that she was made to repeat Sioux words, in a Hopi ceremony, performed by a self proclaimed Blackfoot Chief!

Chapter 6

She, like most of the people who attended these things, didn't seem to realize that every Indian culture has its own sacred and special things. The idea that every individual tribe has their own unique ceremonies seemed to be a foreign concept to her and the others who attended these conferences. Even more strange a concept is the idea that these ceremonies cannot be purchased. They are not for sale.

How pitiful, I thought. My co-worker, like the other people who went to these events, really didn't want to hurt the Native people they mimicked. They were just searching for a way that was right for them. Unfortunately, my co-worker and those like her really didn't want to take the time and effort to get to know a real culture of people. Instead, they wanted an instant connection to something that was familiar to them. She was comfortable with the idea of a medicine wheel representing the Greek zodiac. To her it made perfect sense, even if it wasn't the truth. Worse yet, it made perfect sense to everyone I worked with.

Finally, I had enough. I couldn't take it anymore and I quit my job. I just couldn't be a part of this any longer. No one listened to my attempts at trying to defend what I couldn't help but feel was the raping of my people, despite the fact that I didn't know who those people were.

My frustrations didn't end when my job ended. The more I looked around, the more I saw what I have come to know are called "plastic medicine men"; especially on the Internet.

WALKING THE RELINQUISHED PATH

Hundreds of websites host their words and agendas, as well as rates and fees.

I hoped beyond hope that this plastic medicine man trend would be short lived and would not do too much harm before people saw through it and walked away. Unfortunately, it was a trend that picked up energy and to this day is inadvertently promoted by the very people it insults and hurts.

After many years of abuse and prejudice, the native peoples of North American became rightfully suspicious of outsiders who came out of the woodwork.

In the nineteen-eighties and nineties the Hollywood and television idea of the nasty, blood thirsty Indian was replaced with the kinder, gentler version. The new Hollywood Indian was the silent guardian of the Earth. He had ultimate wisdom and perfection of both soul and body. He came to symbolize, for many, the answer to the modern world we created. The new stereotype certainly embodied all my previous co-workers thoughts of what Native Americans were all about. As a matter of fact, they believed it was the only thing they were about.

It was as if people looked at their crowded cities and shopping malls; they looked at their jobs and their obligations; they looked at the crime and filth all around them, and they longed to return to a simpler time when the world was green with grass and trees, not gray with asphalt and buildings. Hollywood Indians must have looked like the key to

Chapter 6

paradise for those seeking a balance of both spirit and nature.

I realized that my previous co-workers were trying to purchase the Hollywood Indian ideal in these conferences and that the plastic medicine men were providing that service.

The true Indian wasn't what they expected or wanted at all. They didn't want to see a people. They didn't want to see the trouble, the pain, and the human aspect of a people. They wanted love, light and perfection. They wanted a saviour race, they didn't want a human race.

The plastic medicine man was easy for them to follow. They didn't have to change their ways too much. They didn't have to think too far, and everything was the way they expected.

I came to realize that the Indian people themselves added to the problem. They, too, saw this new plastic medicine man trend and became afraid that they would be overcome by outsiders who would further dilute their culture with the plastic medicine man's lies. To many of them, the new-agers and plastic medicine men represented a very real attack on their culture and religion.

Historically, most tribes have always been very quiet about their spiritual beliefs. They hold them very sacred, and sacred things are not to be spread around without regard.

Therefore, since the true Indian people were not rushing to 'fill the market' — so to speak — with the truth, it left a gap for the fakes to fill.

WALKING THE RELINQUISHED PATH

You can't blame the native people for not wanting to spread their idea of spirituality around. Why would they want to trust others with something so sacred. We forget that it was not very long ago that it was common belief that the Native Americans were not even human beings. This fact was supported with twisted biblical scriptures.

The United States President, Theodore Roosevelt, is quoted saying in the non-fiction book, **Bad Lands** by Hermann Hagedorn, (Boston: Houghton Mifflin, 1921), "I don't go so far as to think that the only good Indians are dead Indians, but I believe nine out of every ten are, and I shouldn't like to inquire too closely into the case of the tenth." He also said of the Indians, "Reckless, revengeful, fiendishly cruel, they rob and murder."

When the President is talking about your people like this just a generation ago, you are not likely to believe in the sincere intentions of everyone coming to you now. It is no wonder that the native people didn't run out with open arms and welcome those coming to them.

It has often been said that American people are not use to waiting. They want what they want now, and by and large they get it, provided they have the money to pay for it.

For the people I knew, money wasn't an object. They were willing and able to pay for anything they wanted. So when authentic Indians were not the Hollywood ideal they were looking for, they ran to the mock Indian spirituality offered by the plastic medicine people.

Chapter 6

Like evangelists of other religions, the plastic medicine men they found promised the goods for a price. The most popular of the ones they followed travelled across the country doing performances for crowds who paid upwards of five-hundred dollars a head to take part in the ceremonies.

I remember the day a co-worker of mine got his totem animal. I came home that day and said to my husband, "What am I struggling for? To heck with thousands of years of tradition. If you can pay for it, you don't have to fast and pray and work for a connection to your totem. The boss just gave that guy he follows a hundred bucks. The guy hummed for a minute, then told the boss he just communicated with the Great Spirit. He said the Great Spirit told him that the boss' totem was an eagle. Then he sold the boss a silver eagle necklace he just happened to have in the back of his car for only a hundred dollars more!"

The most frustrating thing of all was that I could see that as these plastic medicine men got rich selling their homogenized version of Indian religion, it made it so much harder for sincere people looking for a true connection to be taken seriously. Even more painful was that the tribes these fakes claimed to represent were hurt in ways that are often hard to realize.

As I see it, the real problem is far more complicated and far more dangerous to the Native peoples of North American than probably anything else they have faced. It is so dangerous, in fact, that some people in different Indian Nations have actually declared war on plastic medicine men and anyone else who is not a full blooded, card carrying member of their tribe who engages in any version of their tribal rituals. Some tribes have gone to great expense and trouble to trademark and/or copyright their sacred ceremonies, words in their language and even their tribal name.

What could be so bad that they would be driven to such extremes? What are they fighting so hard to save? Surely it's not just the right to be the only ones on Earth selling dreamcatchers.

The most horrifying thing these plastic medicine men are doing is perpetuating a stereotype created by Hollywood from the very start. The stereotype would have us believe that no matter if you think Indians are blood-thirsty savages, or angelic guardians of the Earth, all Indians are the same. They are one people. They all live in teepees, wear big feathered head-dresses and moreover, they all believe exactly the same thing.

The plastic medicine men would have us all believe that there is only one kind of Indian. And in most cases, the plastic medicine man wants his audience to believe that one kind of Indian is the ideal of whatever his current audience is looking for. If the audience he is 'working' all seem to be wearing crystals, suddenly he knows a Sioux based crystal ceremony. If he discovers the next audience is made up of devoted believers in Jesus, he will have another supposed authentic Jesus themed ceremony of some other tribe at the next stop.

Chapter 6

From what I have learned, I believe that the people who attend these things truly believe with a sincere heart and purpose that they have paid for the truth. Most are not well read on true Indian culture and few really know any Indian's who live on reservations or in traditional ways. Some of them wouldn't know a Hoop Dance from a Bar Mitzvah. They have no frame of reference to see through the fakes in front of them. They just know they expect to pay the money and come out feeling better, and they do.

But they come out with more. They come out believing that what they just experienced is what it means to be Indian. They come out believing that the fantasy, the play, the performance they just took part in represents all there is to know about the culture and beliefs of hundreds of individual tribes whose history goes back thousands of years.

To them, there is no difference between a Pennacook and an Inuit in culture or belief. They learn to believe that all Indian cultures are the same. Moreover, because these ceremonies are geared to their own pre-conceived, non-native belief system, they develop an even more jaded view of their already narrow perspectives of Indian Spirituality.

The big fear, as I understand it, is that as this false view grows, soon it becomes so strong, that like the Hollywood Indian did so many times before, it will overtake the truth and the truth will be lost forever.

Native peoples fought so hard to keep the shreds of their individual cultures alive. It is no wonder the idea of non-Indians performing their ceremonies makes them feel as if the white man has come back to take what is left of them. A Hopi man once said to me, "Since he couldn't kill all our bodies, he's decided to try and kill our souls."

It makes me very sad to say that I can see his point. But the truth as I see it is that if the indigenous people would reach out to correct the stereotypes and teach the ways they hold dear correctly, it would greatly help. The only people who can ultimately prove that Kickapoo and Narragansett beliefs are not exactly the same are the Kickapoo and Narragansett people themselves.

I began by asking what is in a name. I found that I am once again asking that question. What is in a name? The answer is more than I imagined.

I know the beliefs, values and culture of different tribes are not the same. How was I to learn more about Native American values and culture without generalizing them and homogenizing their spirituality?

I realized I couldn't say I was Indian. I had to say I was this or that kind of Indian. Knowing I had native blood wasn't enough. I had to know where it connected to, now more than ever before.

So, there I was in the time of the plastic medicine man; without a job and without a tribal name. Worse yet, I knew that even if I found who the tribe was, if I could not produce a series of birth certificates that matched some name on their rolls that connected me, I would just have my

Chapter 6

grandfather's word and a handful of circumstantial evidence. That wasn't good enough. I was sure people in the tribal offices would not believe my story of my grandfather's blood, not with all the others coming back to them to be part of the Indian fad. How could I prove that I wasn't looking for my roots for the same questionable reasons some of those around me were. How could I show that I was not one of those people who believed that the total of being a Native American meant having the word eagle or hawk in my e-mail address.

If I told them of my dreams and how they have been driving me since I was a small child, how could I hope to stand out from those around me who were going into Tribal offices claiming to be the reincarnation of Pontiac, Sitting Bull or Crazy Horse?

I knew I had not jumped on the bandwagon. This was not something new for me. To find this out and connect with my people had been a quest I had been on since I was a small child. But if I ever found my people, how could I make them know this?

Chapter 7
Wings of White Eagle

All my previous encounters with self-proclaimed medicine people were at the least very uncomfortable, even hurtful. The months on the job with the followers of the plastic medicine men, and the consistent road blocks and occasional snubbing I encountered when I called tribal offices looking for information, not to mention my grandfather's years of warnings, had tainted my attitude. I was just about at the point where I was starting to believe my grandfather was right, that my people would only spit on me if I ever found them.

In desperation, I called my friend Donna who lived in South Dakota near several Indian reservations. I asked her if she would help me connect to some of the people there so that they might be able to help me find my family roots. I had never talked to her about the Native Americans near her hometown. I had never talked to her about any natives at all, so it was difficult for me to bring up the subject. It was even more difficult to listen to her reply.

"Why do you want to get involved with those people?" she said. "They are the worst bunch of drunks and thieves; every last one of them. They

Chapter 7

come into town, get drunk and break up the place. They rob people blind!"

"Oh, come on. You can't judge a whole people by a few bad apples," I argued.

"Well," she said, "you've always been a good friend to me and you know I would do anything for you. But I'm not going to talk to them for you, for your own good!" She took a breath and continued with a stern and steady tone, "Believe me. If you are one of them, you don't want to tell anyone. They are all drunks and thieves. People will think you are, too. Besides," she continued, "if any Indian tells you that you're welcome, they are only saying that because they want to get close enough to rob you!"

I couldn't believe what I was hearing. She was an echo of my grandfather! How could this be the truth? I was not so naive to believe that they were a people without problems. I knew that many tribes had high alcohol abuse and suicide rates. I knew that many tribes had high crime rates, but I saw this as more of a reflection of the poverty and hopelessness they were made to suffer. Like any depressed population, their is bound to be higher rates of crime in their neighborhoods. Nevertheless, just like in other depressed populations, it was likely that the troubles were caused by a few radical elements, but the majority of the people were good people living in a hard place.

Her words about the Native American people depressed me more than you could imagine. I reasoned that it was her skewed opinion talking and that she couldn't be right. Still, I began to feel the old pains of my childhood again. The more I thought about what she said, the more I thought about my grandmother telling me she would never have married my grandfather had she known he was an Indian no matter what her feelings for him were. I wondered if the whole non-native world were divided into two camps: The Indians are no good drunks and thieves camp and the Indians are the new-age saviours of the world camp.

At this point, I entered a long period of feeling like my search was hopeless. I was even beginning to feel bitter that it looked like the whole of creation was against my finding out who I was. It was at this terrible low point in my quest that I met White Eagle.

My husband and I were on our journey looking for answers to the questions that drive us forward, when we chanced to meet an old man who was a member of the Hopi people. He was a quiet man, soft spoken with a strong, deep laugh that could shake leaves from the trees. Even at seventy years old, he stood more than six feet five inches tall. He was a tall man by any standards, and particularly tall for the Hopi people he hails from. His name was White Eagle.

White Eagle was really what he claimed to be. He was indeed a recognized Hopi Indian who grew up on the Mesas the Hopi occupy, still lived in the area and followed traditional ways.

What I found refreshing about White Eagle was that he didn't know a darn thing about chakras,

Chapter 7

soul power polarization, psychic shields or magical celtic stones. He was like no one I had ever spoken to about Indian beliefs before.

The summer before we met White Eagle, my husband, Paul, and I went up to visit a Mohawk medicine man and his family on a reserve in Canada. My husband knew them quiet well, but this was my first time meeting these people. Paul had told them all about me and about my dreams and my search for my roots. He even told them that I may have had Mohawk ties, based on my Uncle Bob's story.

The woman and her children made me feel welcome, but her husband said very little to me. He just stared at me like he didn't appreciate my visiting his home. I don't believe he said two words to me the whole time we were there. His wife must have sensed my uneasiness, and she teased her husband with a big mexican hat, trying to get him to lighten up and laugh. Though he laughed and talked to everyone else, he just stared silently at me as if my chair was empty and he was looking at a picture on the wall behind me.

When we left, my husband Paul explained that this was the way of the medicine people he had met on the reservation. "When they meet you, they are quiet and thoughtful," he said, adding "You shouldn't worry about it." Still, I did. I couldn't help it. I felt that if this was the way I was going to be treated by friends of my husband who knew I was looking for my roots, how would medicine people who were total strangers treat me?

WALKING THE RELINQUISHED PATH

That was one reason why meeting White Eagle was so important in my life. White Eagle never made me feel like I owed him anything, or like I had three heads. He never stared at me or made me feel ashamed of myself. He never accused me of trying to steal his culture or being a wannabe Indian. When I dared to tell White Eagle about my dreams, he listened with interest. He didn't doubt my words nor did he ignore me. He even suggested what some of my dreams could mean, based on his culture. He always pointed out that I needed to find my people and interpret my dreams by their standards.

White Eagle was never upset when I asked questions, no matter how obscure or personal. His answers were down to Earth and matter-of-fact. Sometimes he was so frank, that I found it a bit uncomfortable.

For example, he told me how he and several others he knew were hired by a company that ran tours through the mesa where his people had a reserve. They hired the people of the tribe to dress in a way that better fit what the tourists expected to see, and walk around the mesa villages doing things people would expect them to do. He said that at times he was hired and paid well to attend functions the tour company put on for their clients. Sometimes he was paid just to ride into town on his old horse to give the place "atmosphere".

He also said that to make extra money, there have been times he set up an outdoor stand in a busy part of a nearby town and made dreamcatchers

Chapter 7

while tourists watched. He told them traditional stories and sold his dreamcatchers to the crowds for a lot more than he would ever get selling them in shops.

He laughs when he tells that story, for as he is quick to point out, Hopi don't traditionally make dreamcatchers. But as he is also quick to point out, the tourists don't care. "They expect to find dreamcatchers for sale where Indians live," he said.

"White Eagle," I asked, "aren't you perpetuating the 'all Indians are the same' stereotype when you sell dreamcatchers?"

"That would be the case if I didn't make a point to tell everyone who buys one that they are not traditionally Hopi," he said. "The people who buy them are happy and it is a nice addition to my little retirement income."

"I suppose if you tell them," I said, but I wasn't sure I totally agreed with his thinking. Nevertheless, he was the one who lived there, so who was I to argue?

Though White Eagle indulges in a bit of commercial gain because of his culture, he draws the line when it comes to what he calls, "fleecing the whites".

He said that there are some Indian people he knows who are so bitter that they delight in doing things they think will cheat non-native people. Though he admits there are a few who talk of serious kinds of hurt, most who talk indulge in simple things. For instance, he knows a Navajo man who buys inexpensive, handmade blankets and rugs

WALKING THE RELINQUISHED PATH

in bulk from China, removes the labels and sells them from roadside stands, shops and markets as genuine Native American made. He gets phenomenal prices for them, too, White Eagle has said.

He also said this Navajo man is not unique. He said there are native people who have the attitude that it is not just okay, but it is an obligation to cheat white people (and non-natives of any skin color) because of how their ancestors were treated. White Eagle believes it is a pointless course that is only going to make things worse.

"It does not make sense to answer evil with evil," he explained. "If you do, before long all that is left is evil."

White Eagle said when he makes dreamcatchers or attends a dinner for tourists in his traditional dress, he is not hurting anyone. He calls these little things he does for money, "playing Indian" and insists he would never do anything to hurt his people. If he felt for even one moment what he was doing was hurting his people, he would stop in a heartbeat.

White Eagle doesn't have to "play Indian", he is an Indian. Just the fact that he feels he has to pretend to be what he really is in order to fit into what tourists expect to see proves that the stereotype of their culture really is an item that the rest in the United States are willing to pay for.

Unfortunately, White Eagle's children and grandchildren are not part of the wanting crowd. He has no one in his family who is interested in

Chapter 7

following in his foot steps. It is an ironic tragedy. His only son, a carpenter, is working hard to put his two sons through law school. One is interested in Native American law issues. The other wants to be as far away from his native roots as possible when he graduates and enters his practice.

I find myself thinking how strange that was and I had to ask, "White Eagle, how can your grandson turn his back on his people and their way of life?"

White Eagle laughed. "How you gonna keep them on the farm?" he asked, singing the old tune that goes with the words. "Our way of life is not what he wants. He wants the big city. He wants the electronic life," he explained with sadness. "You know, there is not a lot for a lawyer to do on the mesa."

"Electronic life," I teased. "You told me you got your granddaughter a Playstation for her birthday. You liked it so much you wanted one yourself!"

White Eagle laughed again. "It's always the way, isn't it," he said referring to his grandson leaving. "You don't know how important what you have is until you throw it away."

He said so much in that one sentence. I wondered if my family never walked away from their native roots, would I have been like his grandson? Would I have willingly — even anxiously — thrown away something I yearn to have so strongly now?

WALKING THE RELINQUISHED PATH

White Eagle often sparked questions in me. He was, and continues to be, one of the best sounding boards I have had when it comes to my native roots.

Still, I know my roots are not Hopi. I know that the one thing I can never learn from White Eagle is the ways and belief of my people.

White Eagle has taught my husband, Paul, and me so much about his people. He also helped us understand a lot more about the nature of his people's belief about the spirit and nature of the Mother Earth.

For example, he wakes each morning and prays to the Sun, thanking the Sun for another day of life.

I asked him, "Why do you worship the Sun? You know it's just a lifeless ball of hydrogen?"

"You think so," he said smugly. "First, I do not worship the Sun itself. I honor the energy, the Spirit that makes the Sun. Everything has an energy and a spirit. It is that essence that I speak to when I speak to the Sun," he explained.

"Second. The Sun is not just a ball of hydrogen. That is only what science tells you. What science can't measure, it can't see. The Sun has an essence I just told you about. It is that essence that makes the Sun alive."

Before this, I was under the misguided impression that he worshiped the disk of the Sun as if it were some supernatural being who has taken on the form of the Sun. I thought it was something like Greek mythology, and the way they worshiped

Chapter 7

heavenly bodies because they were said to be Gods forced into star and planet forms.

But this was different. This wasn't the worship of some deity in Sun form. This wasn't even worship in the terms I had come to understand it with my Catholic upbringing. This was the acknowledgment of a spirit and energy that fueled a living part of a living creation.

Did my tribe think that way? After all, White Eagle could only tell me what Hopi believed and what they did. Could I assume, if I dared, that my tribe — whoever they were — would think the same way?

Paul and I learned a lot from White Eagle. But because he lives so far away, we only see him for short times now and again. In many ways, White Eagle is my first traditional contact with any native culture.

He has been an example for me. He has also reaffirmed both my hopes and my fears.

He has confirmed the fear I have that some Indian people are very negative towards the descendants of those who left their tribes, some are very bitter towards those who are not Indians, and those who are only partial blooded. His stories gave credence to my grandfather's warning about not being accepted by the people his family left behind.

Not all that White Eagle said was negative. He told me of many people who, like himself, think that it is a good thing that the "lost children" — as he once put it — are coming back to find their true ways.

WALKING THE RELINQUISHED PATH

He has been accepting and supportive of me in my search. He has also been very accepting of my husband who has little, if any, real Native blood in his veins.

White Eagle said that it is not your blood that makes you an Indian, so much as it is your soul.

Still, for all his support, White Eagle could not help me find my people. For all the kind words about the soul, not the blood making you an Indian, I would need a solid connection to find out who I really was. Though to this day White Eagle has been a great source of information and inspiration, he has not been able to do much to help me find that connection.

What I can thank him for is helping me to feel more comfortable with a people who often seem so far away.

After getting to know White Eagle, I never again doubted that there were more than two types of Indians. Finally, I could forever put to rest the polarized view others had tried to impress on me that all Indians were either charlatans and fakes trying to con money out of unsuspecting middle aged housewives, or drunks and thieves out to riot and break up the civilized world. I knew there were real people with full, rounded personalities, values and brains living behind the false labels applied to them by years of prejudice and ignorance.

For this I have to thank White Eagle.

Chapter 8
The Internet Path

As I continued my searching, I found that because of my time and resources, most of my research needed to be done on the World Wide Web. Not to my surprise, I found the web to be a confusing and very unwelcoming place at times.

I started with genealogy sites. I found many on the web, but almost all of them charged more money to access their records than I had. I had already spent thousands ordering records from places via regular mail. For all the money I spent, and all the letters I wrote, I found that most of the paperwork I received was useless to me. Sometimes it wasn't even what I requested.

Because of this, I wasn't very motivated to spend hundreds of dollars more to purchase access to websites that promised to have records of my ancestors.

I found a few free sites, but they never had anything about my family on them. It seemed most of those sites were filled with information given to them by others who already had researched their roots. I guessed that no one but me had any interest in my family. A few sites I found told me they had death, birth and other records of the names I put into

WALKING THE RELINQUISHED PATH

their search engines, but in order to reach these records I had to subscribe to their service. The cost for these subscriptions was beyond my price range.

I decided to try and search any and all websites hosted by any of the tribes who lived in the area where my grandfather was born.

Months and months of searching only made me so depressed I felt like giving up.

One night I dreamed I was standing in a field. A tall native man was standing there, too. He was leaning on a very tall, wide, old, oak tree. I felt like this was the same tree that drank me up when I was rain in my previous dream. The man stood there and looked down at me, as he was so very tall.

He said nothing. I looked around and saw the whole glade was filled with the most amazing white animals. There were white wolves, deer, moose, even what I was sure was a white tiger. The whole thing was amazing to behold. I stood and watched in wonder. I didn't know at the time that this was to be the first of many dreams where I would meet this Indian man in a field full of white animals. In future dreams he would speak with me.

That morning, still reeling from the dream, I started my web search with new hope. I came to a website that seemed encouraging. It had a lot of information about the people and the site gave me a welcoming feeling. There were stories on the site about people who came back to the tribe and there was even a story about how the site's webmaster had traced his roots back to his people.

Chapter 8

I felt like it was fate that I should find this site after such an intense and powerful dream the night before, so I decided to write the webmaster a letter. If anyone would understand what I was going through, he would, I believed.

I told him about my grandfather, and about my search. I told him about my uncle Bob and the Mohawk. I told him almost everything. I didn't tell him about the dreams, or even mention the dream from the night before.

I waited anxiously for a reply. Finally, one came. It was not what I expected at all. The letter was rude. More than rude, it was down right nasty. It accused me of being a "wannabe Indian". The man said there has never ever been any Indians named Shaughnessy and that I should face the fact that with a name like that, our family wasn't Indian, we were Irish. And to go bother someone else.

His exact words were, "Go steal someone elses' (expletive) religion!"

I was in shock. How could he write to me, a total stranger, with such hatred and anger? I re-read my original letter two or three times, looking for anything I could have said to insult or upset this man. There was nothing I could see in it that would even be deemed questionable. Surely there was nothing that would invoke such a strong reaction in this man.

I was even more shocked because I assumed that the dream I had the night before was some kind of indication or promise that this would be a valid connection for me.

WALKING THE RELINQUISHED PATH

I wrote several letters in reply to this rude fellow's letter to me, but in the end, decided not to give him any more fuel to insult and hurt me and never sent a reply. I took his website off my Internet bookmarks and never returned there.

My search continued.

I finally broke down and paid to get into one of the genealogy websites, only to find that Canadian records were not one of the databases they stored yet. Nevertheless, in the small time I was with them, I did connect with a woman who had some Canadian records from her search. She gave me a website location, where I found my grandfather's family listed on an old census.

The information was scant, but it did give me a location. I began to contact local authorities looking for more records.

In the meantime, my depression over the type of websites I was finding on the Internet grew. It seemed that all the sites I found fell into one of five basic types.

The first was the new-age plastic medicine type. Hundreds of sites on the Internet were full of people who claimed to be medicine men and were selling everything from past life regressions to psychic healings. For a price, these people would take you on spiritual retreats and get you in touch with your "inner Indian".

The second type were the ones that strived to educate the public on such things as language or crafts. I found that many of these sites were simply

Chapter 8

front doors for the sale of language tapes and dictionaries. Nevertheless, some were interesting.

The third type of sites I found were what I called the "art war sites". It almost became comical to me how hot and nasty the interactions could be concerning these sites. The first of these sites were run by brokers or artists selling Native American made artwork and crafts. The objects on these sites were usually very beautiful, but rather high priced for my wallet. For example, on these sites you could get a painting of an Indian Chief and an eagle done by a real Indian artist. Or, if your wallet couldn't handle the price, you could go visit the other extreme of the "art war sites". On these sites, you could get a painting of an Indian Chief and an eagle done by a non-native artist. These Native-theme paintings done by non-natives are usually, but not always, far less expensive than the ones done by card-carrying Indians. Thus the war begins.

Soon you find the third type of site involved in this group. On these sites, you have long and often vicious ravings in defense of the Native American artist, claiming that the non-native people have no right to paint Chiefs and eagles, as these are spiritual symbols. Of course, the other side has its own war sites, which are often just as vicious, saying that the only reason the Indians are upset is because the non-Indians sell more paintings for cheaper prices.

These types of arguments made me wonder if there was any point in going further with my search. What stupid things to be fighting over. To me, it did not seem to be an issue. If I were wealthy enough to purchase a handmade painting of a Indian Chief and an eagle, I would purchase the one that I liked best. My decision would be based on what sang to me, not what nationality the painter was.

The fourth type of site I found were tribal information sites. There were few of these, and for the most part they really didn't have a lot of information for the public. Most of them were working sites for the people who lived on the reservations. I found these sites very interesting as they were a window into the every day life of the people living on the reserves they represented, but they were not really helpful in my search.

The last type of website disturbed me even more than the plastic medicine man sites. These were the militant Indian sites.

I found far too many sites that listed a declaration of war on white people for stealing the Indian culture. I found many sites that were dedicated to discouraging people from finding their Indian roots by calling them outsiders, unwanted and wannabes.

There were so few sites where I could actually learn anything about the Indian peoples of different nations.

One afternoon, I was talking to my husband, Paul, about how wonderful it was that we found White Eagle and how lucky we were to have at least one contact. I complained to him about all the things I was finding on the Internet. I told him that there were very few sites out there where a person could

Chapter 8

learn about the spiritual ways of the different Native peoples from the people themselves.

Paul mentioned that White Eagle would be a great source of information if he had a website. We talked some more and before long the Voices of the Earth website was born at the internet address —
http://www.earthvoices.org .

We started the site as a place where Native Elders who wished to teach could post their words and essays for the world to see. It started with the words of White Eagle. He thought it was such a great idea, he contacted others he knew and soon we had several Medicine People, Tribal Elders and others writing essays for our site.

The site was a wonderful thing that grew from there. We were contacted by Elders of other Nations and peoples. We were even contacted by a Tibetan Monk who gave us articles about his views and beliefs.

I wanted to post his articles because they were very interesting, but couldn't really put up the Monk's words with those of Native American's. Paul and I wanted to have a separation between non-native and native ideologies, so we started a section on the website called "Voices of the Spirits".

Over the two years we have been hosting the site, more and more people have come forward to offer us material. We always check out the source of the material before we post it.

People love the site. We get thousands of visitors each year, and hundreds of comments in a year. Of the last 300 or more comments, all but one were wonderful and supportive. The one that was not, is worthy of mention because it was supposed to have come from a "real" Indian Chief who did not feel compelled to give us a name we could verify. He claimed our site was a "wannabe" site filled with lies and false plastic medicine man's stories. He claimed our site was on a wall of shame for being one of the sites making money by raping Native American culture.

I guess he didn't notice that our site is 100% not for profit and has never made even one penny. We ask nothing, nor do we even accept donations. (We have turned them away!)

I had to mention the comment here, because when I read the comment I was shocked. It was painful for me to think that someone believed I was raping the Native American culture because my husband and I started a website where we give Native Elders free webspace to post their messages to the world.

I was insulted that whoever wrote this letter simply assumed that the native people who we gave space to were plastic medicine men.

But most cutting of all, he accused me directly of making a web site that would make every person who visited it believe that all Indians are the same.

Of all the things for him to say, nothing could have been more untrue or more hurtful to me. I don't just know in my head, I understand in my heart, that not all Indian's are the same. I also know that every culture has a different belief. I knew this

Chapter 8

when Paul and I started the site. This is why we always make sure that each Native American author has his or her tribal affiliation listed at the beginning of his or her page.

This person seemed to take great offense with one of the authors, a Sioux medicine man named Tantaka. Tantaka is a man who is deeply spiritual, and in his way, he seeks out visions of wisdom. He shared several of these visions with us on the site.

It seems that the sender of the e-mail was insulted by the idea that Tantaka talked about having visions. He even went on to say that if Tantaka was a "real Indian" he would be laughed out of the tribe for having visions. That it was just some wannabe Indian's way of trying to prove they were special.

This nasty and scathing e-mail found my mail box at a terrible time in my life. I was just beginning to find my strength to face the fact that I may never learn what my true ancestry was. I also was trying to face the dreams I had been having.

Only weeks before this letter came in, I dreamed the following two dreams.

In the first dream, I was flying above a large body of water. I saw an island and I came to land on that island. In front of me lay a big hill. On top of the hill stood a native man. He was naked from head to toe. His body was heavily tattooed and he held a spear with a white fur attached to it. He told me to look for my people on the hill where he stood. He said it was the hill where the warriors were buried.

WALKING THE RELINQUISHED PATH

A few days later, I saw the same man in another dream. This time he stood face to face with me. He looked me in the eyes and declared, "The thunder comes before the rain!" With his words, there was an ear splitting crack of thunder and then I felt pouring rain on my face. I woke with a start, expecting to find that the roof in the bedroom was leaking, pouring rain on me, but nothing was wrong.

Having these types of dream-visions was not unusual for me, but it was very painful. I never knew how to classify them and didn't know what to make of them. I have been embarrassed to have them and am often afraid to tell people about them at the risk of sounding like a nut.

Then, that nasty e-mail came in. I knew that it was likely just written by someone who had a chip on their shoulder or one of those people who put up websites declaring war on whites and anyone not living on a reservation who even says the word "Indian". But it did rattle me, because it voiced an inner fear I had. Would people think I was nuts because of my dreams? Would they think I was another wannabe making up dreams to try and prove they are part of a tribe?

Although I knew the e-mail was not important, and I knew from the hundreds and hundreds of positive comments we got that this was just somebody with a personal problem they needed to work out, I couldn't let it go. It plagued me.

I thought about putting some kind of disclaimer on the site saying that though Paul and I were not card carrying Natives recognized by any

Chapter 8

particular tribe. The words on the website were not our own, and that we did our best to make sure everyone who posted as an Indian was, in fact, what they claimed to be.

Paul pointed out that I was overdoing it. The site clearly states who everyone is and that I needed to let it go. Besides, the comment about the visions wasn't even directed to me. It was directed to Tantaka.

I knew what I had to do. I called Tantaka and read him the letter. He laughed and said, "Someone on a long walk with a stone in his shoe, eh?"

I read the part of the e-mail that was a nasty comment about Tantaka's visions again and he simply said, "The visions I have are between me and which ever spirit chooses to give me the vision. Maybe he doesn't understand this yet. Maybe he's just a bit jealous because he's not grown enough to be given visions of his own, yet."

"Yet?" I asked.

"Yeah," Tantaka said, "when a man is growing, there is a point between being a student and being a teacher where he is a jerk. He thinks he's the teacher and he knows everything. He believes if it doesn't happen to him, it is not possible. It is his lesson to learn. He will make lots of noise and make a lot of people who are learning unhappy by his ignorance. But to those who have been there already, we look at him and just let him be. We know he's just making growing noises. If he stays true to himself, he will get past it and someday know. Just ignore him," he said. "The guy who wrote this message thinks he knows it all, and that proves he's still has so much to learn."

Tantaka's words were comforting to me. Still, the issue of visions bothered me.

"Tantaka, why do some people have visions and other people don't?" I asked.

"I don't know," he said. "Some people have them because they quest for them, I suppose."

"But how about those who don't seek them out, but they happen anyway?" I asked.

"Those people don't have a choice," he said. "Those people must have some powerful ancestors looking over their shoulder, directing and advising them."

I asked, "How do you know what a dream or vision means?"

"There are some people in some tribes who understand the symbols of the dreams of their people. For example, to some tribes to dream of an owl means someone in your home is soon to die. But to others, it is an omen of good luck," he chuckled. "You know, to some tribes it's just a dream about an owl. Some bands, over time, have lost their traditional way of dream interpretation."

I dared to tell him of the dream I had of the man with the tattoos on the hill of warriors.

"You are being called by your ancestors," he said. "Maybe they know you are looking for them and they are giving you clues to your path."

Chapter 8

"Why?" I said quietly. "If I find them because of clues from dreams no one is going to believe me."

"Maybe not. Especially if you don't believe you," he said firmly.

"I don't believe me?" I echoed. "I believe me. I do believe me!" I insisted. "I know what I experienced. I know I have had these visions happen to me at times when I was wide awake. I know I don't drink. I don't take drugs. I don't do anything chemical to alter my mind. I know these things happened and they are real, not creations from drugs or alcohol!" I argued.

"I believe you," he said. "I know what it is to have visions. It is my experience that for every one who believes you, there will be many who will not believe you. If your insecurity puts you among those who doubt, you will never learn from your visions."

He was right. I had such fear of the visions I was having and how they would make me appear in the eyes of others, that I tried to ignore them and turn my back on them. I was so afraid of what "real Indians" would think of my visions that by the very nature of my thinking, I excluded myself from ever finding my native roots. By worrying in such a way and to such an extent, I created a break between me and "real Indians". I was unconsciously labeling myself an 'outsider' by virtue of my fear of what those on the 'inside' would think of me, a self labeled "unreal Indian". After all, if I were not "real" in my own heart, how could I ever be "real" in anyone else's eyes.

It was at this point I decided to pay more attention to my dreams and visions of a Native theme. I resolved to try and ignore anyone who called me a wannabe Indian. I knew I wasn't a wannabe. I was an Indian by my birthright and blood. I couldn't change that, no more than my grandfather could change the fact that he didn't want to be an Indian.

Considering Tantaka's words, I decided to try and find the "hill where the warriors are buried" on an island somewhere in Canada.

It didn't take long before I found that there was an island where the Great Lakes met in Canada called Manatoulin Island. I also found that there was a place on the Island that was considered sacred to the Natives there. It was a large rock on the top of a big hill where they once buried their warriors, Chiefs and others of notable actions. The rock, now called Dreamer's Rock, that sits at the top of the hill has become a popular tourist attraction according to the websites I visited. In the past, it was considered a very sacred place. Young men and sometimes women would travel to the top of the hill and sit on the rock, praying and fasting for days. They would then be given a vision by the spirits to help them shape their life.

Sometimes they would see their totem; that is, an animal or plant spirit who had chosen them. This totem would assist them, lead them, and help them much in the same way some modern Christians believe guardian angels do.

Sometimes they were given a vision that directed them to go on a quest. It seemed that visions where not unheard of by the people who lived on Manatoulin Island. There were three tribes of people who lived on the island and all three took part in these vision quests.

So, if I were to believe in my own vision, then I had to conclude that my people were from one of the three tribes who lived on Manatoulin Island. I was either Ojibwa, Odawa or Potawatomi. Collectively, these people called themselves the Anishinabe.

Anishinabe was a name I had heard about. An Elder from the Anishinabe wrote an article for the Earth Voices website. When we checked his references, it turned out that he was an Ojibwa from Canada, but did not live on the Island. He wrote the following for the website. As I read his words again, I became encouraged that this man might have some answers for me.

What he said is written below. You can also find it on the web at:

http://www.earthvoices.org/mg012001.html

Misskwa Geesis
Jan 20, 2001

The Mother calls me Misskwa Geesis. I am an old man from the people called Anishinabe. I was given a copy of the great words of Brother White Eagle and it touched my heart. I came to this place and read the words of many great Brothers and Sisters from many nations and I felt compelled to add my humble voice to those here.

I find great importance in what is being done on this website. I know, as Brother White Eagle and others have suggested in their words, that many Natives are bitter about sharing their culture with the white brother. This is just the opposite from everything I believe. It is very different from the lessons taught to the Anishinabe by the Neegawnnakayg (seers) and from the truth in the times of the Seven Fires.

All who are alive today are the people of the Seventh Fire. So I extend to those Native Elders and Medicine People a challenge to heed the words of the Neegawnnakyg and sit by the seventh fire with an open heart so the good future of the eighth fire will come.

Perhaps you do not know about the many fire's man has sat by. Please allow me to humbly tell you what I know of such things.

A long, long time ago, seven Neegawnnakyg came to my people. They came to us because we were living in peace and they knew we would listen. They told us of seven very different times that our people would see. These times became known as the seven fires. I do not know their exact words

Chapter 8

by heart, but I will tell you what I know in the best words I have. And I will tell you how each of the first six has come to pass. Now we are in the time of the seventh, and possibly last, fire.

The first Neegawnnakyg came with the First Fire. He said that our people would rise up and support the Midewinwin Lodge. Midewinwin Lodge is of Medicine teachers. Our people will become strong under their guidance and they will lead us to a promised land where we would be safe. If we stayed where we were, we would be destroyed. We were told that someday we would find a place where the food grew on the water, but there would be many stopping places before we got there. One of these places was on big water. We stopped there for a long time and there was much happiness and peace in the time of the first fire.

The second Neegawnnakyg spoke of the Second Fire and said that when the people lived by the big water, they would have such abundance they would forget the good the Midewinwin did. They would become lazy and ways of the Midewinwin would be forgotten. This happened. But a boy was born who helped the people get back on track. He made them start to move again.

The third Neegawnnakyg told of the Third Fire as the time when the people find the land where the food grows on water and they settle there. They did.

These three fires document my people's quest for a stable place to live, inland, by large fresh water. Once we lived on the northeastern seacoast in what is now the United States.

The Fourth Fire was given to the people by two Neegawnnakyg who came as one being. They told us of the coming of the white man who would be wearing on their faces their intentions. If their faces showed the face of brotherhood, there would be peace and wonderful times for all. They would bring knowledge to us and learn knowledge from us and all will be good. If they are true brothers, they will come bearing only their open hearts and hands, and carry no weapons.

But if their faces are wearing the face of death, then beware. If they carry weapons, even if they talk like brothers, they are trying to hide the face of death. They will almost destroy the balance of life for the people and all but destroy the cup of life with sickness and murder.

We know, sadly, that when the white man came, they brought weapons. They did not wear the face of brotherhood and the cup that held life was almost spilled empty for Native peoples. The pain and suffering caused is well known today.

Chapter 8

The Neegawnnakyg of the Fifth Fire told of white people coming with news of great joy; talking of God and salvation. They will promise all peoples such joy with this salvation that many will follow them. This will destroy the people more than any physical sickness, because it will cause many to leave their traditional ways and follow the white man's ways. It would destroy not just bands and tribes, but families will be torn apart. It would be an underhanded attack that would be sure and lasting in its pain.

Sadly, this too, came to pass. The white people, most of whom believed they were doing the best for the Native people, brought their religions to our people. The pain and the atrocities of their "gift" and how they imposed that gift are too long to say at this time.

The Sixth Neegawnnakyg talked of the Sixth Fire time that would come because of the Fifth Fire burning so strongly. He told of a time when the children and grandchildren would turn their backs on their Elders. They would reject the teachings of the Elders and the traditional ways as being stupid and useless. They would leave their tribes and families and not return. They would not respect the ways or the keepers of those ways. They would loose all sense of value for who and what they are.

WALKING THE RELINQUISHED PATH

Sadly, this too came to pass. As more and more Native peoples were taught white man's religion and culture, they were also taught to be ashamed of their own heritage. The children and grandchildren came to believe that it was wrong to be Anishinabe (and many other tribes, too.) They were ashamed of their blood and ran away from it in all ways they could. They no longer kept the sacred ways. They forgot their connection to the Mother. The ways of the people would have dissolved to dust if it were not for a few strong souls who kept the thread alive.

This time came. This time is just ending.

The Time of the Seventh Fire is the most important time of all because it is the time we are living in and it is the time of talking. It is the time that I humbly implore all Elders to consider before they turn their backs on their wayward children.

The seventh Neegawnnakyg told of the time of the Seventh Fire. In this time, the wayward grandchildren and their children would be blessed with the wisdom to know that they are not wholly as the Mother and the Creator wants them to be. They may not have much, if any Native blood in their veins, but they will have the Native spirit in their hearts. They will feel the value of what their parents and grandparents threw away. They will try and retrace the footsteps of their

Chapter 8

grandparents. They will come back to the Elders who held the thread of truth and ask to be shown the old ways.

The Neegawnnakyg said that the Elders will be in a spiritual sleep and will not recognize their grandchildren. Neegawnnakyg called these children the "New People", but the Elders will call them the enemy. They will accuse the new people who return of wanting only to hurt them again. Many will believe the new people are only wearing a false face of brotherhood in order to return and destroy what remains of the Native People. They will refuse to believe that it is in these new people that the future will be coming.

This is where we are today. I see so many Native people unable to let go [of] their bitterness long enough to see that they are being asked to re-light the fires of their ancestors. It is a hard job to love your enemy. But the Neegawnnakyg tell us that if we do that, good things will happen. For one, we will find that they are not the enemy, but the future.

So what comes next? The Neegawnnakyg of the Seventh Fire said that there are two paths that could happen at this point. Only one leads to the Eighth Fire.

The path that does not is one where the New People will be foolish in their ways and be forced to give up in their quest. They will be disrespectful in the way they approach, so the Elders will never hear them and will not wake from their selfish sleep. Then the time of the Eighth Fire will never come.

Maybe this means life for all people will end. It at least means that time for the Anishinabe people will end.

The path that leads to the Eighth Fire is one that will be very difficult for the New People. It is one that will truly test their hearts. They must first find the respectful and careful way to approach the Elders. They must be sure to give them the great respect they deserve, not just for being Elders, but even more for holding the thread of truth alive for so long.

They must be persistent and follow the sound of the Water Drum, even when they are turned away. And even if the Elders never wake up and take their proper place as teachers and "parents" to these people, they must never give up in their quest to find the old ways and live by them. They must follow the sound of the Water Drum and it will bring them once again to the feet of the door of the true Midewinwin Lodge. The path to the Midewinwin Lodge is not gone forever. It is merely overgrown. A true heart can find it.

When the new people find it, the heart of the Native people will once again beat strong. With the patient guidance of the Elders who know the truth, these new people will be eager to learn what the Creator wants

Chapter 8

and live the way the Great Spirit intended man to live.

Only in this way will there be true peace again.

So, with all my heart, I call to my Brothers and Sisters from all Tribes, Bands and Nations. Do not turn your heads and close your hearts on those who come to you with sincere intentions. It was written so many, many centuries ago that this would happen. It is as it should be. Let us rejoice in our once naughty children coming home with their hearts now open, rather than to close the hut and refuse to let them back.

His words were an inspiration to me. I tried to contact him to speak to him about what he said, but was unable to track him down.

I was disappointed to say the least, but hung on to the hope that maybe his words reflected a greater majority of people who would welcome the sincere back to the old ways.

I began to read everything I could about the Anashinabe, hoping something in the books I read and websites I visited would ring a bell in me. There was not a lot written about the Anashinabe as a whole, but I did manage to find a substantial amount of information about the Ojibwa people. It was very interesting, but nothing really seemed to hit home. Nothing triggered the memories of the stories my grandfather told me. I wasn't sure anything could bring back those memories, they were so long forgotten.

They say history is written by the victors, and I have never seen this so well played out as in the writings of the colonial settlers with concern to the Indian people. I read books about Ojbwa history only to find that very little, if anything, existed about these noble people before the white man. The books were all about the killing of this or that Indian man or woman. They were filled with stories from the European settlers' perspectives of how savage and dishonest the Indians were.

Whenever they dared to give the Indians any credit for their achievements, they spoke of their brilliance and understanding as if it were not human intelligence, but rather some animal instinct.

These books were so full of such terrible stories that I would open them randomly, set my finger down and begin to read. When I did, without fail, I would find a story about some evil savage being killed.

I didn't know what was worse, the old books written by Europeans full of horrible wrongs they inflicted on the Native people of America, or today's websites filled with hatred and calls for revenge posted by the decedents of those who were wronged.

Chapter 9
The Connection

My grandfather can be as tight lipped as a clam! Much to my despair, it seemed as if he would never give me a crumb of a clue to help me. Then, when I wasn't expecting it, either his heart softened a bit, or his "too old to remember" game failed him for a few brief moments and he gave me just enough information to let me move forward again.

It was on Thanksgiving day in 1999; my whole family got together at my sister's house. The dinner at her house was pleasant and everyone had a nice time. My grandfather was his usual self and refused to talk about anything even remotely involving his past, no matter how much my sister and I asked.

When we were leaving, my sister mentioned that she had some items she wanted us to take home with us. She was going to be moving soon and could not take them with her. The items included a large grill and some furniture. We packed all we could into my parent's van, but there was no place for my grandfather to sit once everything was inside the vehicle. This meant that my grandfather had to

WALKING THE RELINQUISHED PATH

make the two hour drive back to his house in my car with my husband, children and me.

We spoke very little for the first half of the trip. The holiday traffic was rather thick and at times we were going at a snail's pace down the highway. Finally, during one of these snail's pace patterns in the traffic, my grandfather said, "Hey, Paul, bet you miss Canada when you have to drive in traffic like this?"

Paul laughed. "Not really, Pipere," he replied. "Traffic in Toronto is a lot worse."

"Oh, you came from Toronto," Pipere said as if it was the first time he was hearing it. "You know, I never really got to Toronto much. I use to live by Lake Nippising you know."

"Really, Pipere," I said with interest. "Where abouts?"

He didn't reply.

"You know, my dad said the fishing is really good on Lake Nippising," Paul said. He went on to talk about some of the other lakes in the area where he visited. "The water is really cold, but the canoeing is wonderful!" Paul finally said.

"Yeah," Pipere said. "You know where the water is really cold. Up by Georgian Bay. It's really cold up there. When I was a boy, my grandmother use to live up that way. She had a small farm. You know in those days people didn't like to farm, but they had to. She had a brother named Charles. He refused to farm. He ended up becoming a minster or something. He ended up living in the church

Chapter 9

because he wouldn't farm. You know they did that in those days."

"He became a minister because he didn't want to farm?" Paul asked. "That's strange."

"What was stranger was that he was a Presbyterian. My grandmother was Catholic. But that was because she was raised by nuns in a Catholic School."

"What was your grandmother's name?" I asked. "What school did she go to?"

"Her name was Newberry. Addy, Adelaide Newberry," he said. "All her kids were Catholic, too.

"I remember my Uncle Charles, her brother. He was all fire and brimstone all the time. I was terrified of him when we were growing up."

"That must have been strange, with your grandmother being Catholic and the rest of the family being Presbyterian," Paul commented. He turned to me and our eyes met. I could see the stress in his face. It was clear he realized that my grandfather was finally opening up about his family for the first time ever and he was afraid he would say the wrong thing and my grandfather would close his mouth and say nothing else as quickly as he began to talk.

"You know, the whole family was Catholic," my grandfather continued. "My grandmother, Newberry, her children Alfred, he was my father, and my aunt Margie and my aunt Clair. They were all Shaughnessys. She had a son named Edward. He was a Newberry, I think. I don't know."

WALKING THE RELINQUISHED PATH

"How come some were Newberry and some were Shaughnessy?" I dared.

"Well, I think she got remarried, but I think she changed her name. My father used the name Shaughnessy cause that was his name. His father was named that. They called him Felix, but I don't think that was his real name. My father's mother starting using Newberry again cause he died and she changed it back," he said. His words almost fumbled as if he were trying to understand it himself.

"It doesn't matter," Pipere continued. "She had a brother named Charles. He wasn't Catholic. He was a Newberry. Maybe the nuns made her change it. I don't know."

"Which nuns?" I dared.

"How would I know. I was just a kid." He turned away from me and looked at the road again. The traffic was thinning out.

My grandfather talked a little more about how he lived in one of the most far northern towns in Ontario when he was a child. He said he lived there for a short time while his father worked building homes for the miners in the area.

Paul and he talked a bit more about the beauty of the lakes and rivers in Canada. Soon the traffic was moving at a quick clip again, and my grandfather returned to quietly watching the road go by his window.

I looked for something to write on, and managed to find a scrap of paper and a pen in my purse. I wrote down the name of his grandmother,

Chapter 9

her brother, and her children. I couldn't remember the name of the town up north. When I asked, my grandfather just ignored me, as if he had shared all the information I was ever going to get from him. I couldn't complain, it was more than I ever got in all my adult life from him.

I returned to the Internet the next day with new information.

After days and days of research, I came across an obscure record on an Ontario government website. It was a notice about the bequeathment of some land in 1898 by a woman named Addy Newberry. The bequeathed property was in Manitowaning, on Manitoulin Island.

Could this woman be my grandfather's grandmother? Could this be proof that my dream about the man with the tattoos and the island where the warriors were buried was really a vision to help me locate my ancestors, as Tantaka had suggested?

I dug a bit deeper and found that the record continued. It said she left her land equally to her brothers Charles and William, and to her sons Alfred and Edward, and her daughters Clara and Margie.

It all fit! I looked on in shock! There they were. Pipere's grandmother's fire and brimstone brother Charles; my grandfather's father — her son Alfred; Edward her other son; and both of the sisters my grandfather named on the trip back from my sister's house.

I called my husband at work. I couldn't contain myself.

WALKING THE RELINQUISHED PATH

"She bequeathed land on Manitoulin Island," he said with amazement. "She must be Native. They were made to live on that Island back then, if my memory serves me right."

I rushed back to the Internet and began to look up the history of Manitowaning. What I found amazed me.

At the time my grandfather's grandmother lived there, Manitowaning was the subject of something called the "Manitowaning Experiment". It was a grand joint undertaking between the government of Canada and the Church at Manitowaning on Manitoulin Island, to turn the Native Indians into "a colony of good, church-going Anglicans, British subjects, and farmers."

Those Indians who resisted farming were forced to live and work for the church in an effort to "civilize them." The also recruited "Indian preachers" to run the church of the colony.

I read more about how the Catholic church soon moved into the picture and opened schools for the Native children, sometimes tearing families across religious lines. This all made sense. It fit. Moreover, it confirmed my vision.

My grandfather's family came from Manitoulin Island, and my vision was of Manitoulin Island. My ancestors really were trying to help me find my way back to them. At least I hoped so.

With new energy, I looked for more information about the Native people of Manitoulin. There were three tribes living there. They were the

Chapter 9

same in many ways, but they were different, too. I needed to know which tribe my roots connected to.

I researched some more and found this entry on a website that listed deaths and wills, Felix Shaughnessy stood at his brother's side and petitioned the church on his brother Thomas' behalf in the month of July in the year of 1887 to allow the burial on Church grounds of a "Icelandic Child of Savage decent." According to record, the child died before baptism and thus was not considered for burial in the church yard. This indicates that Felix Shaughnessy's brother, Thomas Shaughnessy, was the father of a child who was considered "Icelandic Savage." This surely meant that he and his brother were Indians, but did this mean he was Inuit? The term Icelandic Savage lead me to believe so. If so, what were they doing living on Manitoulin Island?

Just about this time, I dug out the old paperwork my aunt June left behind. Once again, I called the church where the paperwork was said to come from. This time I got a reply.

The woman I spoke to was very nice and in just a few short days she faxed me copies of all the paperwork the church had on my grandfather's family. This consisted of six baptism certificates.

I watched each certificate as it printed out from the fax machine, quickly reading each line as it became visible. The first two copies of the original certificates coming across my fax machine clearly displayed the surname Chatigney! What struck me almost immediately was the fact that aunt June was not crazy. I was momentarily overcome with sadness that she was treated so poorly by her brothers and sisters before her death because she stuck to the story that the family's last name was really Chatigney. All the time they knew that it was the truth. Even my grandfather must have known.

I took a moment to acknowledge to the spirit of my Aunt June, my ancestor, that I found the truth and had the proof to vindicate her. Immediately, I was overcome with a strong sense that I needed to call her son, Jim, about what I found.

Before the faxes were all in, I was on the phone to Jim. He and I both experienced the same strange sense of relief as I read him his mother's baptism certificate. It was as if my Aunt June's spirit was finally at rest.

Before I was off the phone with Jim, all six faxes were done printing. Of the six, there were three which seemed to have the surname Shaughnessy, each spelled differently. One was spelled Shaughnessy, the next Shawunasse, the last Shanessy. Of the three named Chatigney, two were spelled this way. One was spelled Chatiney.

What was amazing was that the names were intermixed. By that, I mean that they didn't use all the Shaughnessy derivatives first then change to Chatigney, but rather the six certificates, when viewed in order, had mixed last names.

What was even more amazing, was that it was clear that the parents were all the same people. Each listed a mother with the last name Lamareaux, with a spelling within one or two letters. But the first name Delima was listed as Mary on one. The

Chapter 9

father was always listed as Alfred, but his last name changed with that of the child.

It was clear they were the same parents for all the children, but why would they change their surname. This confused me, especially when the six children were all baptized in the same church. The Church would have had records of the names of their parishioners. How could they just walk in and tell the church they were named Chatigney and even baptize their child with that name, only to come back a mere year later claiming their name to be Shaughnessy and baptize their next child under that name?

I called the church. The woman explained that records were not taken very well back then, but the fact that my family changed their name often suggested they were not European in decent.

I asked, "So this would be more commonly seen in families of native backgrounds."

She answered, "Yes. Back then many natives changed their names. The priest of those days use to change their names for them, too, sometimes. I wouldn't worry about it." She said, "It is clear they are the same family."

"I'm not worried that they may have had different parents," I explained. "I am looking for my tribal connection. If they were Indians, I would like to see some proof in writing that says what kind they were."

"Oh, we wouldn't have those records. Back then they didn't talk about those things. They never wrote them down. They called the Indians savages.

WALKING THE RELINQUISHED PATH

When savages passed the test and joined the church, they were given new names and they were told never to talk about their Indian names again," she explained. "I guess a lot of family history has been forever lost," she added quietly.

"Yeah, I guess so," I said sadly. I thanked her for all her efforts and hung up the phone.

So, I knew that my grandfather's grandmother once owned land in Manitowaning. She willed it to her brothers and children, including my grandfather's father. There was public record of that. If I could find out exactly where that land was, I could find out what reservation it was on and thus find my people. Then I hoped it would be only a matter of a little research to make the connection between my grandfather's baptism paperwork and the people there; thus finding my lost family.

I returned to my computer. It had only been a matter of weeks since I visited the Ontario records Government run site, but unfortunately when I clicked on my Internet bookmark to return there, I found that they were no longer allowing free Internet access to the site. If you wanted a record, you had to hire a person on their staff to research it for you. Or, if you had a microfilm number, you could purchase a copy of that film. I didn't have the money to do either.

I decided that with some luck, and with the baptism certificates in hand, maybe I could find something about the Lamaroux side of the family in the meantime.

Chapter 9

I found the following entry. Hepolite (Paul) Lamareaux, my grandfather's mother's grandfather was recorded as being born on or about 1780 in Quebec on "unsettled land". I found another vague reference in an old cemetery listing that said Paul Lamareaux was allowed to marry in the church as a "Christian Savage". The record was not clear if it referred to the Paul Lamareaux who was related to me, but the dates were right.

I read that it was not uncommon for Indian's who joined a church to be given birth records and marriage records like this. Regardless of my excitement over finding it, this record didn't tell me much of anything.

That night as I sat on the end of my bed and before I even closed my eyes, I had a vision. A tall man stood in front of me. He said he was the holder of the thread. This caught my ear because I had read the word 'thread' in the writing of the Anishanabe man. I second guessed that I was likely dreaming this because of that word. Then he said, "You are a Trader."

"What? What did I do? How am I a traitor?" I asked through my quickly growing fear. I became terrified that he was going to tell me exactly what my grandfather said they would tell me; that my family were splitters and turned their backs on their people.

"Your people were called Traders by the others because they traveled from place to place and made trade," he said.

WALKING THE RELINQUISHED PATH

"Who are they?" I asked with a sigh of relief.

"They once carried the news from tribe to tribe. Now they carry the thread of knowledge and peace," he said.

"Who are they?" I asked again. "Who are they, exactly?"

"We are Odawa," he said. "Your elders will tell you this."

The vision ended and I found myself sitting up on my bed.

"Odawa," I said with surprise. I never thought about the Odawa. Of the three tribes on Manatoulin Island, the Odawa were the smallest. There was so little written about them, there was precious little in the way of census or family names at all.

I thought for a moment, "If this vision was right, why couldn't I be Ojibwa? At least if I were Ojibwa I could find more information about my people."

What was I thinking? I quickly stopped myself. Had I actually found my people? Was I Odawa?

I tried to look up the tribal surnames of the Odawa people on Manitoulin Island. I found a small list of a few names, but nothing resembling Shaugnessy, Chatigney or even Newberry was on it.

Weeks went by without any confirmation that my vision was real. In the meantime, I tried to find information on the Odawa people. There was so little. I found a few references to them on the odd

Chapter 9

page in old books about other tribes. Other than that, the only thing I found was different tellings of the conflict that became known as Pontiac's War.

Pontiac was probably the only Odawa person recorded in history that I could find. It was as if history only recalled the Odawa as a sidebar to the Ojibwa tribe. But from the little bit I did manage to find, it was clear that the two tribes had to be different, or living together for so long they would have become one tribe.

They were a nomadic people. One thing about the Odawa that was different from the Ojibwa was they were just about always moving. Most of the tribes around them seemed to settle in one spot, a few moved in the summer and winter. But the Odawa seemed to always be on the move.

The little bit of their history and spiritual practices I found indicated that they were a very spiritual people. They believed in one supreme being, which surprised the missionaries of the time. They also believed in lessor spirits who involved themselves with the workings of the Earth. Nothing was just a rock or a river to the Odawa people. There was an energy spirit that gave a sense of life and consciousness to all things, called Manitou.

Unfortunately, the few writings I found on the subject of their spiritual belief were written by Christian missionaries and priests who used the examples solely as a tool to ridicule the belief of the people.

There was little, if anything, written about what they believed before the Christians came in and forced their ways on them. There was even less written about their way of life: what they did on a daily basis; how they fed and clothed themselves; how they raised their children. All these things were forgotten by history. This made me very sad. I wished I could go back in time and learn these things, remember them and bring them to this day.

I became even more sad when I found so few sites about the Odawa people on the Internet. Though all the sites I found were at least civil, most were even welcoming, I was disheartened to learn from these sites that so little of their history remained after the attack on their people by the British, more than 300 years ago, that today their people know very little of the old ways. They borrow a lot of their tribal knowledge from the Ojibwa and the Potowatomi who they now consider sister tribes.

I read a story of how in colonial times the British feared the Odawa more than any other tribe because they were the tribe that could — by virtue of their trade relationships with all other tribes — unite all the Indian Nations into one force against the British. Because of this, the British concentrated their efforts on killing the Odawa people. Before the start of the barbaric British campaign, the people of the Odawa Nation numbered in the hundreds of thousands. In just one years time, they numbered less than two thousand.

Though the numbers seem extreme, no matter where I read the story, it was always the same. Though the number might be a bit different

Chapter 9

from telling to telling, the facts indicated that in one year, more than 90% of the people of the Odawa Nation were gone. With them went their stories, medicine, culture, everything. As I read these stories, I could feel the pain of the people, my people.

Still, I didn't have more than a vision to prove to me I was Odawa. The vision said that I would get confirmation from my Elders. It was awhile in coming.

Some weeks later, I was talking to Jim about his mother, June. I asked him if he knew anything else about the people she came from. He said he knew she told him many times, but he just couldn't remember what it was. I asked him if it was Ojibwa. He said, "No." Then he said, "I think it started with O".

I said, "Could it be Odawa?"

He thought for a moment and said, "You mean Ottawa?"

I said, "Yes. That is one way to pronounce it."

He said, "You know it could be. I think so. Yes, that was it. It was Ottawa. I remember because I knew it reminded me of a city."

It wasn't the type of confirmation I was expecting. After all, there were a lot of cities named after Indian tribes and words, and it did take some leading on my part for me to get him to agree to the name.

I decided to take my chances, and talk to my grandfather about it. The next time I saw him, he was visiting my parents to play cards with them. I asked the same question I asked many times before, "Pipere, I think I found our tribe. Will you tell me if I'm right?"

He groaned a bit, as if to say, "Not again." He put his cards down and turned his attention to me.

In the past, for example, when I asked him if we were Mohawk, he seemed slightly amused and said, "No" without much fuss. So it was for my asking if we were Iroquois and several other tribes, too. This time was different.

"I did some research. I found some records and I talked to Jim. I think I found out for sure this time," I announced.

Pipere just grunted as if to say, "Get on with it, I have a card game waiting!"

"We are Odawa, aren't we?" I announced happily, naively expecting my grandfather to join in and joyously confirm my guess.

"I don't know what you are talking about!" he said in a voice that was unlike him. His words shook with each syllable he said. "Why do you bother me with such stuff. We are not Odawa, Ottawa or Yodawa Indians! We are not even Indians! So leave me play my cards!" he snapped.

My mother was even taken back by his attitude. "Pa," she said with a sense of shock that was clear in her tone of voice, "What's wrong?" She motioned with her eyes for him to look at me.

"Nothing," he mumbled. "I don't know why she has to go and start trouble like that. Now she's

Chapter 9

going to think she can just go walk into some reservation and set up her own teepee or something, for Christ sake!" he complained. "Why did I ever have to go and tell her anything anyway?" he mumbled.

"You going to sit there and grumble or you going to play cards, Fred?" My father broke in and saved the day. "It's your turn, you know."

Thankfully, my grandfather turned his attention away from me and back to his cards.

I walked into the living room and sat down to think about what just happened. A few moments later my mother walked into the room to tell me that she felt that I hit a deep nerve with my grandfather. She said that he continued to complain about my digging into the bones in the family basement and how it was not going to do me any good to know what the tribe was.

I said, "Mom, are you telling me he admitted we were Odawa?"

"I think so," she said. "Maybe."

"Mom, this is really important to me. Did he say we were Odawa?" I pushed.

"Well, not in those exact words. But he did say that he was upset that you found out about it. So what do you think that means?"

She was right. Why would he react in such a way if his secret had not been revealed? Was this the confirmation I was supposed to get from my Elders?

I had a hard time sleeping that night. I wondered all night long what I would do next if it was confirmed that my people were truly the Odawa.

The next day I got a letter in the mail from my aunt June's son, Jim. He was thanking me for my phone call about his mother and sending him copies of the paperwork. I gave him a quick call to see how he was doing.

He told me that he spoke to his daughter about things. He said she remembered Aunt June telling her that their people were Ottawa people. But she thought it meant that they came from the city of Ottawa. She didn't know there was a tribe by that name.

Was this another confirmation? It wasn't as unquestionable as one in ink on paper, but it was another confirming statement, albeit circumstantial.

Later that week, my uncle Jim called me back. He said that he talked to my grandfather's sister, Mary, and mentioned to her that I believed the family were Odawa Indians. Mary said, "Well, the cat's out of the bag. Don't tell Fred I told you so."

So now I knew, we were Odawa. Much later, months after aunt Mary's admission, my grandfather finally broke down and confirmed this for me.

I resolved to look closer at the Odawa and learn about my roots. I found a website hosted by the Odawa Friendship Center and a website called the Waganakising Odawa Education Page. Both sites had a very warm and welcoming feeling. There was as much information on the site as I had ever seen for the Odawa people. I had not contacted

Chapter 9

any website since the nasty scathing I received from the webmaster at the site that talked about finding Indian roots that I contacted months before.

My hands shook when I typed up a letter and sent it on its way into the ether of the Internet. The letter was long and detailed. Eventually it ended with the following paragraph:

> ...I realize that you probably have a lot of people come to you asking for advice and claiming heritage, thus, I will understand if you do not have the time or the will to help me. But if you do, I will be eternally grateful to you. Even more so than I am grateful already for what I have learned about our people on your website.
>
> Thank you for your time,
> Michelle Wedel

I hit the send button and prepared myself for another disappointment. I couldn't sleep all night. I was too worried that I might have done something wrong by sending the letter. Did I say something I shouldn't have? Did I just give another person fuel to call me a wannabe.

I could think of nothing else but checking my e-mail to see if there was a reply. I held my breath each time I picked up my mail. The total terror I felt as I saw the reply in my mail box was so unreasonable that I almost dared not to open the e-mail. Finally, after a few deep breaths, I clicked on the mail and it opened.

WALKING THE RELINQUISHED PATH

To my utter surprise, I got a very nice reply to my letter. The man who sent me the reply was to the point and very helpful. He told me that he sent my letter on to several other people who might be able to help me. I received a letter from both of those people before the day was out.

The first was a young man who was a student at a university on the west coast. He seemed very sweet and made me feel welcome. It seemed that he was once on my end of the tracks. He, too, felt compelled to return to his aboriginal ancestral roots and found his way back to his people.

The second was from a woman who was about my age. She, too, was very nice. Her letters were so supportive and comforting that I felt like she was a long lost sister from the very start. She gave me some places to start looking and I began my search looking through old Indian census records of the Odawa people, looking for my ancestors names.

I was very encouraged to hear from her that there were many Shaughnessy's in the tribe on the reservation where she came from.

I was so happy and excited. I finally felt like I was nearing my home. All I had to do was find a link between even one of those Shaughnessys and my grandfather's family, and I could show a link to me.

Unfortunately, all of the spellings of Shaughnessy on the old census rolls were different. They sounded the same, but were different in spelling. Moreover, they were in American tribes,

Chapter 9

not Canadian ones. Worse, none of the first names matched. This was not surprising, considering all the different names on the baptism certificates I had and the fact that my grandfather and his siblings each had at least three given names before their multiple surnames. It was also not surprising considering that there was no set way to spell anything back then, especially in a native language like Odawa which has a lot of dropped vowel sounds.

No matter how hard I looked, I could not find any record showing an exact match to anyone I could claim a direct relationship to.

This led me to a very strange place in my life. I finally knew who my people were. I have no doubt in my mind this day that I am Odawa, 1/4 by blood and more by heart. I have no doubt that there is a reason why I have been drawn so strongly to find my roots and rejoin with them. Nevertheless, I was also overcome with the realization that no matter how much circumstantial evidence I find to prove to myself who my people are, unless some records are found in some dusty archive somewhere that no one knows exist today that can prove it, I have no way of showing the world who I am.

"Why is that so important?" I asked myself. I found myself struggling with the question. Did I really need some kind of paper to prove who I was? Would that paper make a darn bit of difference in who I am? Was there something else I wanted, but didn't know or wouldn't admit to myself?

Chapter 10
Real Indian

I searched my soul for a long time. I couldn't see why rather than being overjoyed that I had found my people and that now I had several friends in the tribe who were welcoming me with open arms, I was feeling more frustrated then ever.

Was it that I was so shallow that I needed a piece of paper to prove I was a 'real Indian'? Was I still so afraid of being labeled a wannabe that I couldn't feel secure in who I was until someone with an official seal certified me?

This didn't make sense at all! I wasn't looking for my roots for recognition. I wasn't looking for my roots for a "real Indian seal of approval". I was looking because my heart drove me to look. I was looking because I had a deep love for the people I looked for. I was looking because I felt like the goal of my search was my home and I had to return.

Now, I was being welcomed back warmly to my people. I must note, of all the people I wrote to, the Odawa were the only ones who were so very kind to me. They understood how I had a need to come back and I was even invited up to spend some time with them in the summer months on our next

Chapter 10

vacation so I could learn more about my people, meet them and share with them. It was everything I wanted since I was a child.

I realized that maybe I was just so long in the search that I was feeling stressed now that the search was more or less over. It was hard to resolve that I would likely never find a direct blood connection because records were so poorly kept, but that I have all moral right to claim my heritage regardless. Because some priest or city clerk didn't spell a name correctly, doesn't make me any less of what I am.

I resolved not to worry about it anymore. I began to try and learn everything I could about the Odawa people and teach my children about them, too.

My husband, Paul, was so supportive and understanding. He was always very interested and now took an active role in trying to learn the specific ways of my people and teach our children about them. He even agreed to spend his vacation taking me and our children up to Canada to visit with the Odawa.

Everything seemed to be perfect, but it wasn't. There was still something inside of me. It was a fear that never went away.

My grandmother use to say, "If a dog bites you, then you will think twice before touching it again." Which is just a different way to say that old cliche' "once bitten, twice shy". I guess I was feeling bitten. Not once bitten, not even twice bitten. I felt chewed up after my long search. I knew it was only a matter of time before I got another nasty letter from someone, who like Tantaka put it, "Was on a long walk with a rock in their shoe."

I knew in my heart it was only a matter of time before someone accused me of stealing their religion or being a wannabe. Oddly enough, I had not gotten over that fear and believed that if I could pull out some kind of proof of lineage or documentation, it would make a difference. I tried to tell myself that I was not feeling that way. I even convinced myself that I had grown out of such insecurities. It wasn't long before I was tested, and I failed.

A friend of mine had sent the link to the website we host, ***Voices of the Earth***, to some man she knows. He visited our site, then wrote her back a very nasty letter which was almost identical to the first one we received at the site months before. He complained about our stealing and raping Native American culture. He ignored the fact that the site is totally free of charge and makes no profit, and accused me of getting rich by being a "fake Indian". He also called me, and everyone who posted on the site, wannabes. He told my friend to tell us to leave the real Indians alone and stop copying them.

He went on about how I was stealing the Indian culture, how I was taking Indian religion and worship and using it for personal monetary gain; and how only "real Indians" were allowed to practice and talk about sacred things.

If you had asked me the day before this letter came in if I were prepared to face the allegations in

Chapter 10

the letter, I would have told you, "yes," with a resounding cry of confidence. Boy, was I surprised by my reaction to the letter.

My first reaction was shock. I didn't know why a friend of mine who knew all I was going through would feel compelled to forward me such a letter. Then I felt shaken and upset that I was once again accused of being a wannabe Indian. At least I thought that was what was upsetting me, but I was wrong.

It was a few days before Christmas. I sat down with my husband and a friend, Jon, who had dropped in for a Christmas visit and we started to talk about the e-mail.

Jon comes from England and is of Scottish and Welsh decent. He has no Indian blood in him whatsoever, yet he has written many songs and poems, some of which have a Native American theme. He even has a website where he sells his music.

I told him about the e-mail my friend forwarded. He could see that it was really upsetting me. He told me a story of something that happened to him that I never knew about before. He said when he was in California, he was asked to play some of his songs for a small college crowd. He was very happy to do so and began to sing some of his most favorite songs. They all had traditional Native American subject matter to them.

I asked him if he wrote them because he liked Indian stuff or if it was because he knew it was popular. I was surprised by his answer.

WALKING THE RELINQUISHED PATH

"I don't write any of my poems or music because I think they will be a commercial success. And though I enjoy the melodic sound of many Native American instruments, I didn't write those songs because of that," he explained. "I wrote those songs and those words because something inside of me wanted to. It was as if the spirit of the music and words had touched me. It inspired me to create. And that is what came from that creative inspiration."

He continued, "What I wanted to explain was when I performed the music in public, at one point a group in the crowd started getting all riled up. I thought at first they were really getting into the music and were dancing along with it, but before long they started throwing things at me and yelling for me to stop."

"Why?" I asked in shock.

"Because, they said that my music was a raping of their culture. They said since I wasn't an Indian, I had no right to sing a song about the Spirit of the Eagle coming to me. They were really more than a tad upset!" he said with his heavy accent. "Kind of like your letter writer."

"What did you do?" I asked.

"I told them," he answered, "that I write what the Spirit directs me to write. My God tells me to write songs as a sort of form of worship, so I do. If my God tells me to build a pyramid or a Mosque to worship, I will. If my God tells me to go to a Synagogue or ring bells to pray, I will; and if my God tells me to burn sweetgrass and sing about the

Chapter 10

Spirit of Eagles to honor creation, I will. Just because your people might have done it first doesn't matter. What I am called to do is between me and my God. It doesn't matter if you did it first."

"What did they say?" I asked.

"Not much really," he said with a smile, "By the time I said all that, security was leading them out."

"Seriously," he continued, "no one owns the Great Spirit! You can't let anyone tell you that you have no right to believe or worship or even think one way or another. Just because you are not a card-carrying, bona fide Apache, doesn't mean that if your path and spirit lead you to worship as they have done, that you are taking anything away from them. How can you take anyone's beliefs away from them?"

He turned to face our Christmas tree. "Just because you believe in Christmas, doesn't make Chanukah any less important to those who follow that way. Just because the guy down the street is celebrating Kwanza doesn't take away from your families joy on Christmas morning, does it?"

"Jon, you are right," I said quietly. "If I never get a paper saying I am Odawa, even if I found that everything I learned so far about my family is wrong and we are Greek or Irish or anything other than Indian, it really doesn't matter. If I believe it is right to do something or believe something, I have every right in the world to do those things."

"Yes," he said.

WALKING THE RELINQUISHED PATH

"But what about people who claim to be bigshot medicine men from all sorts of tribes and they charge people money to learn and do Native-like things?" I asked, "How is that different from you selling a tape of your Native-like song, or some guy selling a painting of an Eagle?"

"This is the difference. You have to be honest with yourself. There are always going to be shysters out there, and there will always be marks to follow them, just begging to get rid of their money," he said. "In my case, I never tell anyone I am an Indian. I'm not. But I will tell them that the Great Spirit moved me to write the music, because the Great Spirit did. And not because I'm an Indian, but because the Great Spirit knows my heart, and my music just came out that way."

"What about people who say if you sing about sacred things, like the Spirit of Eagles, you are desecrating their religion?" I asked.

"How can putting anything to the music from your soul be desecration? I challenge any Spirit to look in my heart and tell me I am doing it wrong by honoring it with music." He laughed, "Hum, I saw a statue of the Virgin Mary standing in a painted bathtub on the lawn down the street. I guess that is someone's idea of honoring her. You see, some people I know back home might find that highly offensive. It is all a matter of perspective."

He was right. The man who wrote that nasty e-mail about our website perceived it as the raping of his culture, but that same website was perceived totally differently by everyone else (but one) who

Chapter 10

has ever written a comment about the site. This made me wonder, was my problem merely one of perspective?

Was it that simple or was there really some hidden moral issue here that I couldn't put my finger on?

"By the way," Jon asked as he was leaving that night. "Why is finding that paperwork so important to you? If you find it are you going to sell your home and move to the reservation? Are you going to start dressing only in traditional ways and only speak the language? Are you going to quit your job and go work for the tribe?"

I slowly shook my head, no. I never even thought of these things before. It wasn't likely I was going to drop everything and move to the reservation if I found a connection. Sure, I wanted to become a useful member of the community, but I never thought about leaving my house and job to do it. So, what did I really need a paper for?

Chapter 11
The Shame in the Shell

For days I thought about my friend's words. I knew that it was very likely if I ever got my official paperwork it would not change anything I was doing or planned to do. I wondered if I had a fear that without some paperwork to prove a direct connection to a tribal member, the people who had been so nice to me would turn their back on me. It didn't seem likely, but maybe I feared this.

Because of this, I wrote to the Odawa woman I was corresponding with and told her that I could not find a direct connection to any name on the role she gave me and my fear that when I visited in the summer, if I didn't have any confirmation or proof of connection, I would not be welcomed.

She wrote back the following:

Of course I'm welcoming you, we're tribal cousins! Plus, not even all those people who stayed in their home communities kept up our traditional ways. Many turned their backs on the culture as resolutely as your people way out in New England. But people will just care about your heart, and clearly you're very dedicated and spiritual.

Chapter 11

You will be welcomed into the Odawa community, ceremonies and sweat lodges. Many here may know your family. Shoot, I think there are even some Shaughnessys and Newberrys in Petoskey.

I was so relieved after reading her e-mail. I could put to rest the idea that the fear I was feeling came from my fear that I would be rejected by the people when I went to meet them.

So then, where was the fear coming from? It was time for a spirit quest of sorts for me. I began a period of soul searching, looking for the key that would open the lock to the puzzle of my fear.

For a long time I prayed to the Great Spirit and my Ancestors to help me understand what this fear in me was. For a long time it seemed like no one was listening.

Then one afternoon, I was sitting at home thinking about things and working on some graphic art for a book cover, when I began to feel very dizzy and disoriented. It was as if my mind was being pulled from my body. I was so dizzy that I checked to see if my baby daughter was alright, in case I passed out. She was playing in the living room quietly. My stomach turned and I decided to rush to the washroom for a much needed break.

As I did, the dizziness became so strong I was overcome with a feeling of spinning at great speed. It stopped suddenly and was gone. But rather than the familiar fish motif of my bathroom, I opened my eyes to find myself looking at the

WALKING THE RELINQUISHED PATH

heavily tattooed man I had seen in other visions. With him stood many other men and women. Most of them had some form of tattooing and bark earrings, like him.

I found myself getting to my feet. Nevertheless, he was still taller than me. He looked at me and said, "I have been watching your struggle. You carry a burden which weighs heavy on your back."

With his words I suddenly felt as if a great weight was physically put on my back. I felt coarse straps around my chest and forehead and I reached to find that I now had a basket strapped to my back. I removed the basket and held it in front of me.

Inside the basket was a shiny surface, like a mirror. As I looked at it, I saw a scene appear. Before I knew it, I was looking at the reenactment of all the terrible atrocities I had read about perpetuated against the Native American people.

I saw children being beaten to the point of unconsciousness for refusing to speak in English. I watched men being ripped apart by animals because they dared to try and defend their wives and daughters against white rapists. I saw people sick and dying from disease as the settlers looked on with satisfaction.

But the most sickening thing I saw was the people I knew were my grandfather's ancestors agreeing to turn their backs on their own people out of fear. I saw them walking away.

Then I saw my grandfather. He was holding a shining sea shell as if it were a bowl. There was

Chapter 11

water in the shell and in the reflection I saw my grandfather's family. My grandfather was a young boy. I saw that there was some complicated problem going on between my grandfather's family and people who had come to them for help. I felt as if I were in my grandfather's shoes as he watched these people, who were family to him, turned away because they had not chosen to conform to the Europeans ways as his own family had.

In that moment of time, I watched and understood that my grandfather was very accustomed to having to turn his back on the family. He was taught to be ashamed of that side of the family. There was a deep and obvious shame he felt when he looked at his uncles, aunts and cousins. There was a feeling in him, even at that young age, that there was something terribly wrong and evil about his relations who were not conforming to the ways of the church. He looked down on them with a sense of contempt, even though he knew they were exactly as he was. There was something else. He felt ashamed of his parents as well. He knew their European way was only a facade. He felt ashamed of himself. As I looked on at the vision unfolding in the shell bowl he held, I saw that as well. Moreover, I felt it.

My grandfather handed me the sea shell bowl and I drank the water out of it. I had no choice. I didn't even think to stop myself. I simply drank it. As I did, I was filled with terrible shame, guilt and pain.

Walking the Relinquished Path

"You carry the shame," the Indian man said. "It is inside of you."

"My grandfather's shame of being Indian." I commented as if I understood.

"You carry the shame of being white," he said firmly. "Your grandfather has given you the shame and you carry it inside yourself. You are ashamed of the choice that was made by your ancestors to be white."

He was right. All this time I was trying to deal with what I thought was a deep down fear of being Indian. Actually, I was ashamed of thinking of myself as white. I thought about all the forms I filled out in my lifetime. I thought about how many times when I was asked on those forms what ethnic origin I was, I filled in Caucasian when I knew full well I was not.

I thought of all the terrible things the whites did to the natives and realized that it was my family who decided to stand with them rather than stand up to them. That shamed me.

That even in my adult life, when my belief in my right to claim my Indian heritage was challenged, I became nervous and upset. That was why I was so sensitive to those who accused me of being a wannabe. I wasn't a wannabe. I was an Odawa. But I reacted on a primal level as if I was a "*NOT wannabe*".

Maybe this was because of the years of conditioning by my grandfather and family. But more, it was because I really was carrying the shame of being white.

Chapter 11

I feared rejection, because I felt as if I could not return to my people or family as a white woman. I had to come back to them as an Odawa woman who had faced the shame and was willing to admit and accept what my family did so long before.

I called my husband and told him about the vision. I could barely talk through my tears. I understood finally what everything meant.

I wasn't looking for a piece of paper, I was looking for absolution. In my mind, that official paper represented a letter that said, "You are forgiven," from the people who my family left out in the cold.

That was why the acceptance I received didn't heal my wounds and fill my soul as it should have. I needed more. I needed to apologize, so that I could then move on. I needed to acknowledge the dishonor my family took part in, and admit that at least one of that family has returned with humility and respect.

A strong new strength filled me. I knew what the next step was. The path I was trying so hard to follow in the dark was finally starting to make some sense.

As strange as it sounds, I finally realized that all the time the only thing holding me back was my own shame. I *was* carrying the guilt for my family.

I contacted the Odawa woman I had been talking to via the Internet once again. This time I told her about my feelings and how I knew I was carrying a guilt about my "white side". I explained to her how I finally came to the realization that my grandfather had impressed the shame on me, and somehow, I had taken that shame and internalized it.

The guilt I was feeling was clear to see from my letter. I didn't know how she was going to react to my letter or what she would write back.

It was a few days before she replied. Each of those days seemed like an eternity. I began to suspect that she had finally had enough of me and had decided not to write back.

When she finally did write back, she said that she understood how I was feeling and that my feelings were common with people in my position. She explained that the main goals of the society of my grandfather's time was to force Indian children to adopt English language and ways through systematically destroying their social structure with tactics that ranged from shame to savage brutality.

She went on to say, *"I know an elder who saw a classmate killed before his very eyes when a teacher beat him for refusing to stop speaking Navajo. Can you imagine such a thing? They buried that poor child in the school graveyard. Didn't even send him home to his people. He was only nine!!"*

She ended her letter by telling me not to worry and saying, *"You will come to know that this is yours now and has always been yours, and is there for your children."*

She was right. It was mine and my children's. It always had been mine, regardless of rules and regulations created by bureaucrats. No matter how many "card-carrying" Indians on reservations called me a wannabe, I knew then that

Chapter 11

I had every right to be a wannabe. I have every right to work and strive and reach until I find my way back on the path my grandfather relinquished. I was a wannabe in the truest sense and it was not a bad thing. I wanted to be what I was meant to be, what I was born as.

I looked in the mirror, my eyes red from the tears that I just cried, and said out loud, "I am an Indian. I am Odawa!" As I spoke the words, for the first time my heart felt them as a burning truth in my being.

Chapter 12
The Gift of the Fox

Something changed in me that day. Something that cannot be explained. I looked out the window to the backyard. The sun seemed to shine brighter and everything seemed to look a little better to me. I looked into the small area of trees behind my home, at the shining water of a nearby pond.

Something moved in the brush. I looked over toward the movement, expecting to see a neighborhood cat. Instead, I saw a beautiful red-tailed fox. It walked out from the brush and into the center of my backyard, well away from the protection of the trees.

This was very odd behavior, considering it was early afternoon, and very sunny out.

I looked at the animal closely. It seemed healthy and aware. It didn't seem sick at all. What would cause a nocturnal animal, like a fox, to come out into an open area in the city in broad daylight?

I rushed to the back door, only half expecting the fox to still be there when I arrived. It was still there. It stood completely still and totally silent, looking right at my house.

Chapter 12

I dared to open the back door. The fox didn't move. I stepped out of the door onto the landing in the back of the house. The fox did not bolt away. It just stood there looking at me.

For a long moment I stood there staring at the beautiful creature. Our eyes met and we locked in what seemed like an eternal gaze. It was as if, for that moment, the fox and I were the only two creatures in all of existence. I felt a strong bond with this animal, though I had never seen it before and had only seen a wild fox one other time in my life.

I felt as if seeing this beautiful fox standing in my yard was a reward of sorts for finally making the heart connection to who I really was. I thanked the Great Spirit for this blessing. When I did, the fox almost seemed to smile at me, or was that just my perception?

It had been at least two full minutes and the fox had not moved. It seemed too trusting, and I began to wonder if I could approach it, maybe even stroke it. I contemplated doing just that when the thought occurred to me that no one would believe me about the beautiful fox in the backyard.

I decided to go back into the house and get my camera. I had to take a photo, if only so I always had the memory. I slowly withdrew into the kitchen and reached over to grab my camera and turn it on. This whole process took less than ten seconds. When I returned to the door, the fox was trotting off towards the pond. I managed to get a photo of the orange and black tip of the animal's tail as it disappeared into the brush.

I kept looking out the windows on that side of the house, hoping the fox would return. Later than evening, I told Paul about the event and he suggested I talk to Ed White Eagle.

I called White Eagle. He suggested that I was being offered "Fox Medicine" and a Totem. He told me the proper way of accepting medicine. He also told me that I would likely be tested soon to see if I were strong enough to claim my heritage.

I asked, "Tested how?"

He did not answer except to say that I would know it only after it was over.

Unfortunately, White Eagle was not in the position where he could come and perform any ceremony for us, and we had no other Medicine connections nearby, so Paul and I did our best to perform the ceremony that White Eagle outlined, including every detail we could.

Our own ceremony was very personal and meaningful. Though it might not have been 'by the book' and some people would even suggest that we had no right performing it at all, we both felt that the Great Spirit was pleased with our efforts, as we came into the ceremony with a clean and open heart.

The morning after the ceremony, the fox returned. I was washing dishes, looking out the kitchen window to the backyard, day-dreaming about anything other than housework, when the fox walked out of the woods. I hurried to the door and slowly and quietly opened it.

Chapter 12

The fox turned and looked me directly in the eyes again. I remembered what White Eagle said about Totems and thanked the fox Manitou for the great gift. The fox actually nodded its head, as if acknowledging my thank you, then trotted off into the woods.

I never saw a fox in the yard again, though I look for one every time I look out the window. But I did see my Totem again. Once again a fox appeared to me as a reward or perhaps a sign post of sorts from the Great Spirit.

It started one afternoon. I was working with a potential client over the phone. He was explaining to me the theme of his upcoming project. He explained he had a little bit of trouble getting some people to co-operate with him, because as he put it, people grouped his work with that of "Damned evil Pagans and Indians". He added. "They don't believe in God, you know. They're all godless, tree worshipping idiots. Did you know that once...."

"Sir," I broke in and cut him off mid-sentence. "I cannot talk for people of all Pagan faiths, nor can I speak for all Native people, but I can speak for myself as an Odawa Indian. I am insulted by your remarks. To assume that every one of a race of people is an evil, Godless idoit, when it is obviously that you know little — if anything at all — about them, is small minded and short sighted.

"I cannot talk for others, but I know that my people and my family are deeply connected to God, The Great Spirit, which ever name you choose. And

WALKING THE RELINQUISHED PATH

I must insist that if you wish to do business with my company you keep your racist attitudes to yourself."

The event went on for several minutes. I was steadfast in my conviction that I was Odawa, and I was not a godless, tree worshipping, idiot."

The details of the event aside, once it was done and over I realized this was the test that White Eagle spoke of.

I stood up to a client who's views belittled the Native American people. More than just stand up to him, I stood up to him as an Odawa Indian. I didn't just say I was, I felt it. When I said, 'my people,' I meant it. I felt the right to defend the people from the inside.

Had this event happened just a few short months before, I know I would have felt awkward and maybe just let the comment slip by with nothing more than a reply like, "Well, we all have different views of the world and God," or "We are each entitled to our own opinion."

But this time I couldn't let it go. This time it was personal.

I was explaining this event to my husband as we drove home from getting groceries at the store. We took the long way home and were coming down a rather busy side street off the main road. I just got to the point where I was explaining how after I hung up the phone, I realized that by standing up to the client, regardless of any potential monetary loss, it was the first time I actually said to anyone else in this entire world, "I am an Odawa Indian."

Chapter 12

"I was tested, just as White Eagle said I would be, and I believed in my heart I passed," I said to Paul.

Just as I spoke those words, we turned a corner on the road and standing right there in front of us, in the middle of the road, in broad daylight was another fox.

Paul quickly stopped the car so as not to hit the animal. The car came within feet of the fox, yet it didn't bolt and run away. Rather, it just stood there looking at the car.

I looked at the animal and made eye contact with it. For what seemed like an unnaturally long time it looked at me then walked to the side of the road. Only after reaching the side of the road did it run away.

I realized that this was yet another confirmation from the Great Spirit that I was on the right path. I broke out into tears of joy. I have tried to put it into words, but it is simply not possible to explain the feelings I was experiencing at that very moment.

I felt like the turning point in my life was sealed. I would not go back. I could not go back. I had claimed my heritage; not on paper, but in a more real way. I was Odawa, and my Fox Totem sent by the Great Spirit confirmed it for me more than any document from any tribe or government could.

Epilogue

I had found the path relinquished by my grandfather. I had fulfilled the dreams of my childhood and was well on my way to re-establishing ties with my people and my long lost family. I was learning the language and reading everything I could about my people, their history, their customs and ways. I had friends in the tribe and had plans to visit with them in the coming summer. It seemed as though my whole world had changed on the day I claimed my heritage.

Yet, what was different? I had the same job. My home was the same. My children, though learning of their people's ways, were not really very much affected by the revelation of my life.

I didn't start dressing traditionally, and even found it harder to wear clothing printed with generic Indian designs. My grandfather's fears that I would want to run off to go live in a wigwam proved to be a great over-estimation.

What did change was mostly internal. I found, each day, I was feeling more and more connected to the people who I hardly knew. I became increasingly drawn to study the old ways, and learn about the history and culture of the Odawa people. Moreover, I found myself compelled to

Epilogue

find a way to assist my people and become a valued member of the tribe and society.

It was obvious, I wasn't going to be able to make any great monetary contribution to their cause. I wasn't a teacher or doctor. I wasn't a lawyer or any type of professional who could assist them in social or legal matters. In fact, the Odawa people never asked me if there was anything I could offer them. They never required me to give them anything but my open heart.

But isn't that the way it is supposed to be when you go home? When you go home, your family welcomes you out of the cold and into their homes, never asking for an admission price, never requiring you pass an entrance exam.

And just like family, when you return, you never have to be asked to carry your weight. You look around and see where the needs are and you help fill those needs with the talents and abilities at your disposal.

There is no more room in my mind for fear of being called a wannabe. There is no more anger in my heart for the lost souls who ambushed me like noisy highwaymen with words of ridicule as I fumbled my way down the relinquished path. There is no more fear of rejection, and no more guilt about my white side either.

The only regret I have, as I follow the path out of the seemingly endless dark forest and into the lighted valley, is that my grandfather makes every effort to let me know he is not pleased with my discovery.

WALKING THE RELINQUISHED PATH

Nevertheless, I believe in the deepest part of my soul, that he is secretly happy that one of his children has returned to the people he once loved. I know this because I saw it in his eyes when I told him the truth about how I was made to feel welcome by the tribe. His eyes could not hide his feelings even though his only comment was to sigh with obvious disapproval and walk away.

Moreover, I saw it in his eyes as I looked into the shell. He felt the same guilt I did. My acceptance was his absolution.

He is Odawa. I am Odawa, too. I know in his own way he is as proud of that fact as I am.

ABOUT THE AUTHOR

Michelle Wedel is the mother of four who lives with her children and husband, Paul, in New Hampshire. She is the author of several acclaimed books in the field of unusual phenomena research, which she wrote with her husband. She has also written a series of fantasies based on some of the unusual stories she has gathered over the years.

Born in Massachusetts. Her father was French Canadian in decent, but her mother's family had a secret. They were not really Irish, French, British or any other of the many nationalities they claimed to be on various documents. They were Native American Indians. It was a secret that was never to be spoken of, but a secret she could not leave alone.

With her dreams fueling an intense need to discover who she was, she began a long and difficult quest for the truth of her origin.

It was this quest that drove her to question reality and explore beyond the limits of modern life.

It wasn't until almost forty years old that Michelle was finally able to put the pieces together and answer the question of her Native American Heritage.

Michelle Would Like to Recommend You Visit the Following Websites:

Voices of the Earth

http://www.earthvoices.org

Voices of the Earth is a not for profit website which gives free webpage space to various Native and non-native Elders, Medicine People and Spiritual Leaders.

For more information on Native American Cultures, art, skills and for links to many Native American sites, check out:

http://www.nativetech.org
and
http://www.greatdreams.com/native.htm

To write the author, please address mail to

Michelle Wedel
P.O. Box 1862
Merrimack, NH 03054

or e-mail
Mwedel@sweetgrasspress.com

A Premiere Publishing Services Company!

Bring YOUR Dream from Manuscript to the GLOBAL MARKET

Find out how easy it is to have your book professionally published and on the world wide market in less time than you think.

Our personal one-on-one service, experienced staff of published authors and designers, and our commitment to the details that will make YOUR BOOK stand out as a **professionally published, high quality product**, makes us better than all the rest!

You put your soul into writing your book, why settle for any less than the best when it comes to bringing your dream to print?

Your book & World Wide Distribution = Success!
http://www.writetoprint.com
or call toll free **1-877-727-7757**
to find out how to make it happen!

www.ingramcontent.com/pod-product-compliance
Lightning Source LLC
Chambersburg PA
CBHW051758040426
42446CB00007B/418